THE CHIFFCHAFF

HAMLYN SPECIES GUIDES

THE CHIFFCHAFF

Peter Clement

HAMLYN

Cover illustration: A Chiffchaff singing in early spring.

First published in 1995 by Hamlyn Limited,
an imprint of Reed Consumer Books Ltd
Michelin House, 81 Fulham Road, London SW3 6RB
and Auckland, Melbourne, Singapore and Toronto

The photographs are copyright and are reproduced by permission of the following:
p 6, p 26 © Goran Ekström (I G Nature & Teknik AB); p 13 © Anthony McGeehan;
p 15, 22 © David M Cottridge; p 31, 39 © Jari Peltomäki; p 46 © J Bateson (English
Nature); p 47, p 51 © Peter Clement; p 70 Roger Tidman; p 78 © Leo Batten;
p 83 © G P Catley; p94, 98, 103 © Roger Wilmshurst; p 110 © Alan Harris;
p111 © Paul Doherty.

ISBN 0 600 57978 6

A CIP catalogue record for this book is available from the British Library

Page design by Jessica Caws
Maps by Louise Griffths
Printed in Hong Kong

CONTENTS

A winter tristis Chiffchaff in northern India. The pale grey-brown tones of the upperparts lack any green tinges.

Series Editor's Foreword

The Chiffchaff has always been one of my favourite birds. For a small, rather insignificant-looking species, it makes a fair impact. In northern Europe, it is the first of the warblers, and indeed, generally the first of all migrants to arrive back on its breeding grounds in spring. Its song is then so striking and unmistakable that the bird's presence could hardly be overlooked, even if the singer itself is not always immediately visible as it repeats its familiar notes from the top of a still leafless tree.

This delicate-looking bird seems in fact to be hardier than many of its close relatives. It does not migrate far when winter approaches, and a good number of Chiffchaffs spend the entire cold months of the year in Britain and Western Europe. In the south of England, I have seen them in ones and twos (occasionally in small groups) when there has been a god covering of snow on the ground, at a time when the very similar Willow Warbler is far to the south, in Africa. Chiffchaffs are also delightful to watch on passage, in small loose flocks or alone, whether passing through river valleys and gardens or in the middle of a desert wadi. They can then be seen just about anywhere, even in the tiniest of city gardens.

In his text, Peter Clement has placed a great deal of emphasis on the identification of this little bird, and with some justification. Although the 'typical' song of the male in spring is unmistakable, at other times the species could easily be confused with a number of its close relatives, the most likely of which is, because of its general abundance, the Willow Warbler. The fine differences, including those relating to behaviour, between the Chiffchaff and other *Phylloscopus* warblers are here explained in great detail: a careful reading of this part of the book will repay the observer's efforts when he or she ventures out in the field in autumn.

On top of this, however, there is the problem of separating one Chiffchaff race from another (some races may visit western Europe from breeding grounds a long way to the east). It is most intriguing that the races have different songs, or 'dialects', in some cases very different from the characteristic 'chiff-chaff', and also that their calls differ to varying degrees. This is, of course, helpful only when the bird is not silent, so we need to learn the exact appearance of all the races; again, the author unravels the complexities involved.

Yet there is much more, besides. For example, I always thought that Chiffchaffs nested on or very close to the ground, but I now learn that they may also sometimes nest higher up – at over 4 m, and in one exceptional case in north Russia even 11 m above the ground! Simple facts such as this make this book enjoyable to read and a mine of information.

David A. Christie

Acknowledgments

I am indebted to all of the following, who have helped provide information, copies of papers or loans of photographs or other material. No book of this nature can be the work of just one person and I should like to express my thanks and gratitude to the following: Kevin Baker, Dr Leo Batten, Tony Clarke, Nick Davidson, Bob Edgar, Pete Ellis, Chris Galey, Alan Harris, Jo Hemmings, John Marchant, Tim Inskipp, Andy Paterson, Deborah Proctor, Gunnlaugur Petursson, Dr Chris Perrins, Marcos Rodrigues, Søreu Sørensen, Dr J. L. Telleria and Michael Wilson, together with Steve Gantlett of *Birding World* and Sheila Cobban of *British Birds*. I should like to thank all of the photographers who supplied copies of their photographs, particularly Nils Andersson, Julian Bateson/English Nature, Dr Leo Batten, Nigel Bean, Graham Catley, Dave Cottridge, Paul Doherty, Bob Edgar, Göran Ekström, Alan Kitson, Chris Knights, Julian Moulton, Jari Peltomaki, Roger Tidman, Arnoud B. van den Berg and Roger Wilmshurst. I am also indebted to Ian Dawson, Malcolm Rush and Linda Birch, the respective librarians at the RSPB, English Nature and the Alexander Library, Edward Grey Institute of Field Ornithology, University of Oxford, for copies of documents and papers.

Grateful thanks are due to David A. Christie, Françoise Morgan and Brian Hillcoat for their translation skills; and to Peter Colston and Michael Walters for access to the Ornithology Collection at the Natural History Museum at Tring. I am particularly indebted to Chris Mead and Bob Edgar, who commented on earlier drafts of several chapters, and I should like to thank the British Trust for Ornithology for permission to reproduce the Atlas map of Chiffchaff from the 1988-91 *Breeding Bird Atlas of Britain and Ireland* and the CBC graph of the population trend; also the editors of the *Birds of the Western Palearctic* for the use of some of their data. Finally, I should like to thank my wife, Angela, for her patience and support during the writing and production of this book; the same also goes to the rest of my family and many friends for their indulgence and support.

1

INTRODUCTION

In the comparatively recent history of man's interest in nature, warblers have always been a source of inspiration and fascination for poets, naturalists and birdwatchers alike. Enthusiasts of all ages and backgrounds, from beginner to expert, have admired the characteristic (if not always melodious) songs of this widespread family of birds. In Britain and Europe one species has, perhaps, attracted more attention and interest than others – the humble Chiffchaff.

The *Phylloscopus* warblers are a group of some 40 species which occur throughout the Palearctic and parts of tropical Africa. They are all small, and vary from green or greenish-yellow through subtle intermediate changes in colour tones to brown (hence the familiar term 'leaf-warblers'); many look extremely similar to each other, or are separated by the presence of wingbars. The Chiffchaff is one of the smaller members of the genus. It breeds across Europe and Asia and winters in Africa and southern Asia, yet is identified primarily (in most of its vast range) by a very characteristic and instantly recognizable feature: its song.

Of all the *Phylloscopus* warblers, the Chiffchaff is widely regarded as a harbinger of spring because of its cheery, lilting and repeated 'chiff-chaff' song. The early naturalist Gilbert White was one of the first to appreciate that there was more than one species of 'willow-wren', the name under which this species, the Willow Warbler and Wood Warbler had been classed. In his letters on the various aspects of *The Natural History of Selborne*, written in the middle of the eighteenth century, he clearly distinguished between the three species principally by their songs, referring to the Chiffchaff as the smallest uncrested wren (to distinguish the three also from the relatively better-known Goldcrest).

The Chiffchaff is almost unique among the passerines in that its vernacular name is a simple onomatopoeic derivation from its repetitive song. Very few other species can claim such a distinction, Twite being perhaps the only other European passerine (non-passerines with onomatopoeic names include: Chough, Cuckoo, Curlew, Hoopoe and Kittiwake). This name derivation is also reflected in the Chiffchaff's German name – zilpzalp, and in the scientific name *collybita*, which has its origins in the Greek *collubistes*, a money-changer, the monotonous song being likened to the sound of someone counting out money. Of the races, *abietinus* is a straight translation meaning made of fir but here taken to mean a bird of fir trees, and *tristis*, means sad, aptly named after the melancholy or plaintive piping call note. The name Chiffchaff was first used by Gilbert White about 1780, prior to which it had been called the Lesser Pettychaps, the Chirper, Huckmuck (a Wiltshire name also applied to the

Willow Warbler) or Miller's Thumb (a Cornish name applied loosely to three or four different species of warblers which are seen crossing the Channel in spring). The name *Phylloscopus* is a straight derivation of the Greek for leaf-explorer.

The life of the Chiffchaff is one of almost constant motion. These are among the most active of birds, eternally geared with a nervous energy to live at a frenetic pace. Only on very cold mornings or when tired migrants on passage are newly arrived after a long flight are they likely to be drowsy or lacking their normal vitality. Almost every waking moment is spent in continual motion, in search of food, a mate, a territory, a nest site, provision for young or a wintering area. This high rate of metabolism requires a constant supply of food and, in company with the other small leaf-warblers and 'crests' (Goldcrest and Firecrest), their lives are, for the greater part, spent foraging and feeding.

The extensive range of the Chiffchaff, from the Canary Islands and more continuously east or north-east from Spain to the Kolyma river in eastern Siberia, covers a wide diversity of tree-covered habitat. In the main it prefers lowland light or open woodland and forests, but as one progresses eastwards, it also occurs widely in conifer forests; in parts of the range it is a bird of parks and large gardens, copses and rows of trees which border roadsides. It is often found in areas also occupied by its very close (and similar-looking) relative the Willow Warbler, but is separated by ecological requirements and occupies a slightly different niche in the habitat. In the north of its range the Chiffchaff is a bird of the taiga, an area of conifers, birches and dwarf willows interrupted by wet or marshy areas and inhabited by very few humans and a seemingly endless summer plague of mosquitos.

In the more montane areas it breeds in the swathes of conifers, at up to 1800 m in the Alps, and east of the Urals it occurs at up to 4500 m. This vast expanse of arboreal habitat is able to supply the abundance of insects that form its diet in the summer, before it retreats southwards at the onset of winter.

The Chiffchaff's winter range extends from parts of central and southern Europe to around the Mediterranean, Arabia, Iran and northern India, North Africa and the oases of the Sahara, and south to the equator down the Rift Valley in Ethiopia. Although a long-distance migrant, very few penetrate the tropical forests and equatorial regions that are the winter home of the more southerly oriented Willow Warbler. Depending on the severity of the winter, considerable (but variable) numbers winter north to southern England and the Low Countries, where they survive on a reduced, but presumably sustainable, diet of winter flies and small beetles. On warm sunny days or in sheltered areas, principally in the frost-free zones, they can often be seen pursuing early flies or taking spiders and, should the warm spell last several days, be persuaded to give, albeit half-heartedly, a brief and faltering burst of song, only to be cut short when the temperature falls again.

In southern Britain, and at other notable wintering pockets in central Europe Chiffchaffs are not exceptional in winter, although, away from any notable source of food-supply such as sewage farms (an increasingly rare habitat), they are likely to be extremely scarce. If the weather in southern Europe is warm in late February and early March the first Chiffchaffs can be expected in Britain and elsewhere in central Europe towards the middle of March, although many birdwatchers will not see them in any numbers until a week or so later, and not before April in northern Scotland and Scandinavia. Progress through Europe is necessarily slow to allow the thawing of frozen breeding areas to produce the first hatches of insects along with the first buds on the saplings.

In the following weeks the trickle of individuals heading north becomes a flow, and the Chiffchaff is joined by its close relative the Willow Warbler with its equally distinctive downward-spiralling song. The journey for some will have been in vain – the weather can often produce a severe last blast, especially in the east, which will preclude many an early venturer's chances of establishing a prime bit of territory. On their journey north, migrant Chiffchaffs can be seen and heard in almost any suitable piece of habitat likely to offer shelter and sustenance for a day or so off course; even town squares and the unlikeliest tiny city gardens have hosted the presence (frequently unsuspected) of the diminutive migrant. In April and May almost any piece of coastal scrub or woodland is likely to be visited by migrants, often in considerable numbers or 'falls' if the right weather conditions prevail. These falls (sometimes in company with other warblers) are often of birds which have crossed many hundreds of miles (including over open sea) in the previous days or nights.

Although initially appearing an unexceptional member of a fairly large genus of very similar-looking birds, the Chiffchaff clearly has a more complex and structured life than is usually appreciated. The following chapters provide a more detailed and informative portrait of one of the more characteristic species of British and European woodlands and set its place in relation to the other members of the *Phylloscopus* genus; its courtship, territorial defence and breeding behaviour, movements, and the factors that affect, govern or control its lifespan. Before doing so, however, it is worth putting the whole family in context before we single out an individual species.

The *Phylloscopus* warblers, or leaf warblers, probably originated in the Himalayas, since this is the main area which they currently occupy. In all, there are now considered to be about 46 species (depending on taxonomic preferences and including those which are resident in tropical Africa), of which about half are found in the main Himalayan ranges or westwards into the Hindu Kush or east into Tibet and north-west China. They are all small (or smallish), highly active, short-billed, tree-loving birds which are either green or brown in plumage with variations of yellow, olive, grey and brown. Some are characterized by certain features such as head-stripes and wingbars (or both), or pale rump bands. Within the family there are several notable groups which look remarkably similar, both in the field and in the hand. One fairly safe method of identification is the song, but with some, notably the Chiffchaff and the Mountain Chiffchaff, the differences between the two may not always be obvious or apparent to the human ear.

2

IDENTIFICATION OF THE CHIFFCHAFF GROUP

Within the *Phylloscopus* genus of small leaf-warblers the Chiffchaff and its very close relative the Willow Warbler occupy a niche somewhere around the middle of the range of variation shown by the genus as a whole. They have neither prominent wingbars or crown-stripes nor other distinguishing features or marks in their plumage, and they are neither the largest nor the smallest members of the group. In size they are perhaps closer to the larger end of the genus, which ranges from the Plain Leaf Warbler, which is no larger than a Goldcrest, to the largest, the Arctic Warbler. However, the Chiffchaff and its near relations are more complicated than they may appear; confusion with several other leaf warblers, particularly in autumn, is a possible trap for the unwary.

In addition to confusion or complications arising with others of the same genus, it must be remembered that within the species itself there is a wide range of variation – this is usually a sign of a successful species which has evolved into geographically recognizable types within certain areas across the range. Not only does this variation involve the plumage of individuals at different times of the year, but across the range of the races there is a high degree of change in colour tones and in the presence or absence of yellow, olive or brown in the plumage. It is, however, generally fair to say that the brightest or the yellowest birds are in the west of the range, while the greyer or more olive-toned birds, which virtually lack any yellow, are at the eastern end of the range. Nevertheless, it is important to realize that, as with virtually all the rules that apply in bird identification, there are no absolute guarantees that this holds true in every case. In all the races of the Chiffchaff, individuals (or groups) occur from time to time which are exceptions to the rule. This makes the Chiffchaff one of the most interesting and challenging species to identify.

The range and diversity in the plumages of the three Chiffchaff races that span the Palearctic not only have led to confusion and misidentification in the field, but have also created problems for taxonomists wishing accurately to define the species' position and to classify it with the rest of its relatives. There have been, and to a certain extent still are, considerable differences of opinion among the various schools of taxonomic thought regarding the names and number of races that make up the Chiffchaff and those species/races which are now classed separately. These differences over where specific diagnosis should be made concern extremely similar species

A fairly typical view of a Chiffchaff: the alert look, the dark eye-stripe and the white crescents below the eye.

(such as Mountain Chiffchaff) which are genetically distinct and currently (but only recently) classified as being separated from the Chiffchaff; or, in another instance, whether there are more finite differences in the races we currently recognize and whether the intermediate race (*'fulvescens'*), between *abietinus* and *tristis*, actually exists or is due in part to the integration of one race with another. This debate reflects an attempt to establish what the bird (and the rest of its genus) has done in historic and evolutionary terms. It is likely that the Mountain Chiffchaff, an extremely similar 'look-alike' of the Chiffchaff, has recently (but many generations ago) broken away, in terms of its habitat and breeding requirements, from the main stock of Chiffchaffs to occupy its own ecological niche.

In this book, I have followed the classification as set out in the master work on the *Phylloscopus* family by Claud Ticehurst in 1938, with the exception of the two races of Mountain Chiffchaff (*sindianus* and *lorenzii*), now widely accepted as a separate species. The Chiffchaff comprises six races which, to the untrained eye, are all very similar to each other.

P. c. collybita

The Chiffchaff most familiar to birdwatchers in Britain and central and southern Europe belongs to the nominate race *collybita*. In spring and summer it has the upperparts (from the forehead to the rump and uppertail-coverts) dull or dingy green, but with a brownish-olive tinge or wash which gives it a duller tone, except for the rump (normally the centre) and uppertail-coverts, which are slightly paler or brighter green. Some birds may also have the crown and nape slightly paler or tinged grey-green. The wing-coverts have dark brown centres, which may appear blackish at a distance, and are broadly fringed with pale olive-green (slightly paler than the upperparts); on most birds, the dark centres of the coverts, with the exception of the two or three small feathers at the bend of the wing which comprise the alula, are rarely visible in spring. The flight feathers are dark brown but appear darker: the inner webs (the broadest part of the feather) are very fine and (in the hand) almost translucent when spread – much more so than on the very similar Willow Warbler; the outer webs (i.e. that part which shows on the closed wing) are finely edged with pale green or olive-green (but on many spring individuals this is absent by the time they have returned to the breeding areas), and only the dark alula, the inner webs of the tertials and the tips of the primaries stand out as being very dark. The underwing-coverts and axillaries are lemon-yellow. The tail is the same dark brown as the flight feathers and all but the central pair of feathers are finely edged paler or light olive-green, more broadly (but only by a millimetre or so) towards the base of the outer tail feathers. Together with the green on edges to the flight feathers, this is often the area of brightest green on the bird.

The face is characterized by a thin pale whitish or whitish-tinged yellow supercilium from the upper lores (on some individuals the supercilia join across the lower forehead/base of the upper mandible) backwards over the eye and the ear-coverts, where it fades. When considering the identification of other *Phylloscopus* warblers, particularly the scarcer (in Britain) or more northerly species, it is important to pay particular attention to the length, colour and definition of the supercilium behind the eye. The lores are usually dark, or can be partially obscured by paler tips but become dark in front of the eye, and this dark colour extends into a fairly thin eye-stripe across the top of the ear-coverts underlining the supercilium. The eye, which often looks large, is dark brown, appearing blackish in the field, but has noticeable white eye-crescents which appear as an incomplete eye-ring, broken at each side by the dark stripe. The cheeks are pale green, as the ear-coverts, or yellowish-green, but, as the feathers have darker bases, they can, close to, appear slightly mottled. The sides of the nape and neck are usually slightly paler green or tinged more yellowish than the upperparts.

The underparts are dull white or off-white, but with the centre and sides of the breast and flanks yellow, washed with buff or a dingy buff tone, the belly slightly whiter, and the lower flanks, thighs and undertail-coverts vary from dull whitish-yellow to biscuit-coloured. The bill is mainly horn-brown, with a pale orange or orange-tinged basal half to the lower mandible which extends finely along the cutting edges of the upper mandible. The legs are thin and spindly, dark brown or greyish-brown, but often appearing blackish in the field; the upper surfaces of the feet are also blackish, but the soles are a contrasting yellowish.

This is the plumage in which most Chiffchaffs appear in Europe and the British Isles in spring and take up territory to breed. During the course of the summer the plumage becomes heavily worn and loses the greener tinge, assuming a duller brownish-olive or greyish-olive on the upperparts (this can result in some birds generally lacking any green or grey-green whilst others may show a slightly paler or yellowish wash); the underparts become dull greyish-white, with very little, if any, yellow showing on the breast or flanks. At this stage the flight and tail feathers are more noticeably brown or paler brown than in spring, with clearly worn or abraded tips; they lack the bright green edges, which are paler or greyish and greatly reduced or entirely absent. Non-breeding birds at this time of

A Chiffchaff in autumn in southern England. Adults and young of the year are in fresh plumage at this time of year.

the year, which may be those in their first summer, are very similar in overall plumage to breeding birds; since they do not suffer the wear and tear on the plumage caused by foraging for and feeding a growing family, however, they maintain a less tarnished look and the greenness of the spring plumage through the summer months.

Following the breeding season, the adults (of all races) undergo a complete moult of their feathers. This can begin as early as the end of June for some birds (mostly non-breeders or failed breeders) and continues through to September (just prior to the autumn departure); for some individuals it can even be prolonged (owing to particular circumstances such as late fledging of second broods) into October. The loss and regrowth of individual feathers is a slow and gradual process, the replacement of the primaries alone taking up to 45 days. At this time of year, approaching late summer or early autumn, there will be noticeable differences between the dull or drab adults which are undergoing the moult and the fresh plumage of the newly fledged young of the year. Moulting birds, however, are generally less easy to see, as they often hide away in sheltered areas of bushes where they can feed unobtrusively and are also better protected from predators. The loss of some of the flight feathers at this stage means that their powers of flight are somewhat diminished, and their chances of escape would be less if their normal levels of activity were maintained.

On first leaving the nest, the juveniles are similar in plumage to the adults but with brown or grey-brown upperparts; the flight feathers are fresh, and the underparts yellowish-white with a dull or dingy buffish wash on the throat and upper breast. In late summer or early autumn, these birds also undergo a partial moult and replace their body feathers. There is a high degree of variation in the extent of the moult among individuals, as they also replace some or all of their median coverts, inner greater coverts and tertials. In the British Isles many will have completed this post-juvenile moult by the middle of August, but it is possible to find some in the middle of September or even at the beginning of October still in the process of completing this moult. The purpose of this moult so soon (about ten weeks) after acquiring their juvenile or first plumage in the nest (which comprises largely of soft or downy feathers) is to allow the bird maximum flight power and range (for its size) and to maintain its body temperature at high levels. The fresh feathers are stronger and are more appropriate for autumn migration, when temperatures will be lower than when the bird fledged.

Following the early autumn moult, both adults and first-year birds are now in fresh plumage. The upperparts, wings and tail are brighter, greener or olive-green, and the birds are then a shade brighter than in the spring. Some individuals may show a paler or yellowish wash, especially on the rump, which may cause some confusion with Bonelli's Warbler. The supercilium is paler than in spring and is tinged with buff behind the eye, and the white eye crescents show up well against the dark eye-stripe and greenish cheeks and ear-coverts. The black or blackish alula is quite prominent on an otherwise plain or uniformly coloured wing and frequently shows a lemon-yellow feather at the bend of the wing (which protrudes from the carpal-joint area of the underwing).

As winter progresses, the plumage becomes slightly worn, a little faded and duller. Some birds show a definite browner tinge to the upperparts, but this is rarely as brown as that in the late breeding season and never as brown or russet-toned as on the vagrant Dusky or Radde's Warblers from central and eastern Asia (for differences from these two species, see below). In late December, January and most of February, the birds undergo a second but only partial moult of the body feathers; also at this time, some, but not all, of the tertials and the central tail feathers (occasionally some of the next-outer feathers, too) are replaced to bring the plumage into its spring freshness – one hesitates in the case of the Chiffchaff to say finery. As Claud Ticehurst noted in his monograph, the extent of this moult is variable and more complete in some than in others; for some it is very slight and probably undetectable in the field. By early spring, adults and the young from the previous breeding season are impossible to tell apart.

P. c. abietinus

In Scandinavia, northern Europe and most of central Russia (CIS), south to the Ukraine and southern Siberia (north and then eastwards of the Black Sea), the nominate race is replaced by the race *abietinus*. Birds of this race appear structurally identical with those of the nominate race but in the hand it will be noticed that the wings can be slightly longer (males 61–68 mm and 56–62 mm) than on *collybita* (57–64 mm and 53–61 mm respectively) and the second primary is also slightly longer. In fresh plumage this race has, on average, paler or colder, greyer (grey-green) upperparts than birds in western Europe and is paler or whiter on the underparts, with fewer (but not entirely absent) buff or yellow tones, particularly on the breast and undertail-coverts. However, there is a clinal variation within this race, from the darkest birds (i.e. those with greatest similarity to nominate individuals) in western Scandinavia to somewhat paler individuals further east. In addition, in the areas where this race overlaps with nominate *collybita* (e.g. in northern Germany and northern Poland), Chiffchaffs show characters of both races and are racially indeterminable.

In spring and summer, the upperparts of true *abietinus* are brownish-olive with a greyish wash, particularly on the crown and mantle; the wing-coverts and edges to the flight feathers have a similar appearance in spring to that in fresh plumage in autumn but variable between different-aged birds, from those showing greatly reduced or no olive-green edges to those (probably adults) with only slightly reduced amounts of olive-green. The supercilium is pale or whitish-yellow, on some well defined (more so than on the nominate race), particularly behind the eye. The cheeks and ear-coverts are paler or mottled dingy buff and whitish tinged with olive or greenish-yellow. The underparts are mainly whitish (whiter than on the nominate race) with only a slight buffish wash, some show fine yellowish streaks on the breast; the flanks are dingy yellow to sandy-buff (often warm in tone) but the vent, thighs and undertail-coverts are pale yellowish-white.

In autumn (mid-September onwards), the upperparts become browner or dull buffish-brown and (on the adults) noticeably paler olive-brown or even olive-green, the latter especially on the rump while the uppertail-coverts and sides to the base of the tail are also fairly bright olive-green; some adults, however, are greyer on the upperparts. Some individuals (both adults and first-years) may also show a faint yellowish or yellowish-buff wash on the throat and upper breast. The bill is mostly black, with a slightly paler base to the lower mandible visible at close range. The legs are dark brown, but slightly darker than birds of the nominate race.

The post-juvenile and post-breeding moult periods are as those for the nominate race (July and August), but, according to Ticehurst, the pre-breeding moult of body feathers in the winter quarters is also usually complete by February and is usually more visible in *abietinus* birds than *collybita*. Svensson (1992) has also noted that very few young *abietinus* from northern Scandinavia renew their tail feathers before the autumn migration but between 10 and 30 per cent return from their winter quarters with these feathers new. Conversely, young birds in central Europe moult more of their greater coverts and the majority from this region replace their central tail feathers before autumn departure.

Because of the great similarity between most individuals (certainly in the west of the range) of *collybita* and *abietinus* it is unlikely, if not impossible (even with birds in the hand), that, outside the breeding and main wintering ranges of *abietinus* individuals can be distinguished with certainty from nominate *collybita*. This is especially true in autumn, when *abietinus* migrates through the south and southwest of the breeding range and occurs alongside birds of the nominate race. Some autumn-plumaged adults of the nominate race are extremely similar to fresh-plumaged immature *abietinus* and it is impossible to be certain of their racial identification. To the experienced ear, the calls of the two races (see chapter 6) can be of only some assistance in distinguishing between the two.

While there is great similarity between individuals of the two races, and caution is advised in the separation of birds in the field, particularly those in eastern Europe from the cross-over areas, extremes of the two are very distinct. In fresh plumage in autumn, the pale tips to the greater coverts (mostly of immature or first-winter birds) are often noticeably pale and suggest a short or indistinct wingbar. This has on a number of occasions led to some confusion with worn-plumage Greenish Warblers (but see below). Eastern Chiffchaffs (the name usually applied to the races *abietinus* and *tristis*) rarely, if ever, have a wingbar as distinct or prominent or as straight as that on Greenish Warblers.

P. c. tristis

To the east of the range of *abietinus* is the 'Siberian' Chiffchaff *P. c. tristis*. This is by far the dullest of the northern Palearctic races, the only yellow in the plumage being restricted to the feather(s) at the bend of the wing and the underwing-coverts. This race can be further divided into two groups, previously separated into *'fulvescens'* and true *tristis*. The former was considered to occupy the area of overlap between *tristis* and *abietinus* (approximately between the Urals and the Yenisei), while true *tristis* occurred east of the Yenisei. It is now widely recognized that there is a high degree of variation within the races and this is particularly true of *tristis*, which includes individuals which have the upperparts greyish to greyish-brown (*'fulvescens'*) and others which are darker. Some taxonomists, largely working from museum specimens, have suggested that the greyer birds are the result of intergrading with *abietinus* (which occurs widely in the area of contact between the two), but others have pointed out that birds of the *'fulvescens'* type can be found throughout the entire range of *tristis*. It is now considered that *tristis* Chiffchaffs are as variable in plumage as those of both the nominate and *abietinus* races, if not more highly so. The race *'fulvescens'* is thus no longer considered valid.

In spring and summer *tristis*, the upperparts are variably buff-brown tinged grey or brown or an intermediate greyish-brown, with an olive tinge to the lower back, rump and uppertail-coverts; on some the olive tinge may be restricted to the rump and uppertail-coverts, while others show a tinge of olive on the mantle and nape and are probably intermediates between *tristis* and *abietinus*. The wing-coverts are brown and on some birds are edged olive-green or slightly paler green, most prominent on both adults and first-year birds in autumn; the alula is plain or dark brown, with bright yellow edges of the underwing-coverts showing – the only yellow in the plumage of this race. The flight feathers and tertials are brown and can be finely edged olive-green; the tail is similar, and some have the bases of the outer feathers narrowly edged pale grey-brown. The supercilium (which

---

Races of the Chiffchaff and Mountain Chiffchaff.

P.c. collybita adult spring/summer

P.c. abietinus adult spring/summer

P.c. collybita dark individual

P.c. abietinus adult autumn/winter

P.c. brehmii adult spring/summer

P.c. tristis adult spring/summer

P.c. tristis adult autumn/winter

P.c. canariensis adult spring/summer

Mountain Chiffchaff

is often longer than on either *collybita* or *abietinus* and extends to the end of the ear-coverts) is thin but defined, and is whitish-buff, and underlined by dark lores and eye-stripe and pale buffish-brown (or mottled darker) cheeks and ear-coverts; the white eye-crescents contrast well against the dark eye-stripe, cheeks and ear-coverts. The underparts are whitish or creamy-white, with a buff or pale buff wash on the breast and flanks.

The legs are black, with dull yellow soles. The bill is mostly black but tends to have a very small or restricted area of pale yellow or pinkish-yellow at the base of the lower mandible, which, at a distance in the field, appears (as with *abietinus*) all black. Some observers have commented that this race, in comparison with nominate and *abietinus*, is somewhat more dumpy and appears to have a slightly uptilted bill and a peaked forehead.

In autumn and early winter the plumage is similar to that in spring and summer, but some show a noticeable greyish cast to the upperparts and a buffish-brown tinge to the rump and uppertail-coverts. The wing and tail feathers have fine pale buff-brown edges; the tips of the flight feathers are visibly pale buff, and the black alula is often underlined by a pale buff or very light yellow feather showing from the underwing. The underwing is variably pale buff to light yellow towards the edge of the wing. The underparts are whitish, with buffish-brown on the sides of the breast or across the lower breast.

In worn plumage (late summer and towards mid-winter), the upperparts of the adults are variably brown or grey-brown and show little or no olive tinge, except on the rump, the edges of the flight feathers and the edges to the base of the tail. The wings and tail are similar in tone to those of *abietinus* and have greenish-olive edges (usually worn down and absent on late winter/early spring individuals). In fresh autumn plumage, first-winter birds have pale buffish (occasionally or rarely whitish) tips to the greater coverts which often form an indistinct pale curved wingbar (more prominent on some individuals than on others), which disappears through wear as the season progresses. The underparts are generally whiter or less buff, but considerable individual variation occurs and some show a deep buff wash on the sides of the breast and flanks; the general whiteness of the underparts could, together with the presence or suggestion of a wingbar, cause confusion with the similar plumage features shown by Greenish and Arctic Warblers.

It should be emphasized that individuals of both *abietinus* and *tristis* can show a wingbar. The former rarely has more than a pale suggestion of a bar, but, while many individuals completely lack a wingbar, some *tristis* have quite a heavily pronounced one. The presence or absence of a wingbar in late autumn or early winter, on either race, is not a diagnostic feature and is totally absent on many birds.

The southern races
Three races occupy small or restricted ranges in Spain, Morocco and parts of Algeria, Tunisia and the Canary Islands. The 'Iberian' Chiffchaff *P. c. brehmii* has dull olive upperparts tinged brownish on the crown and olive-green on the mantle, rump and uppertail-coverts; the flight feathers and

tail are brown, with olive-green edges to the secondaries and base of the tail. In general it is brighter yellowish-olive than the nominate race, with a greener rump and uppertail-coverts; the supercilium is also comparatively yellower and the cheeks and ear-coverts are mottled with olive or dull yellow. The underparts are deeper, more primrose-yellow, particularly on the vent and thighs to the undertail-coverts and on the underwing-coverts, the throat and sides of the breast are tinged with buff, the belly is white.

First-year birds in autumn are similar to adults but have bright greenish-olive upperparts; some have darker or browner heads. The rump and uppertail-coverts and sides to the base of the tail are bright greenish-olive, as are the edges (narrowly) to the flight feathers. The bend of the wing and the underwing-coverts are bright yellow. The chin and throat are off-white, usually becoming pale yellow on the breast, the flanks are dingy yellow and the belly is whitish; the undertail-coverts are yellow or pale yellow. Both adults and young have brown or pale brown legs and feet.

The two races on the Canaries are similar to the nominate race. *P. c. canariensis* is similar to summer-plumaged (i.e. duller or slightly worn) *collybita*, but differs most notably in being very slightly, but very visibly longer-billed (by a few millimetres). Spring birds have dark brownish-olive upperparts becoming greenish-olive on the lower back, rump and uppertail-coverts; the edges to the flight feathers and base of the tail are light green to greenish-olive. The fairly long supercilium is pale whitish-yellow, while the cheeks and ear-coverts are olive or dull brownish-olive, mottled paler. The chin and throat are off-white, becoming dingy yellow on the lower throat and breast and tinged with dull buffish-brown on the lower breast and belly; the flanks are warm buff, the centre of belly to undertail-coverts pale yellowish white, and the thighs greenish-olive or tinged with yellow.

First-year birds are the same as the adults except that they have some yellow tips to the buff feathers of the breast. The winter plumage is the same as that in summer apart from a degree of wear and the fact that the green on the rump, uppertail-coverts and edges to the flight feathers and tail is paler. The colour of the legs is also more variable in this race than in any of the others, ranging from greenish to grey, brown or yellowish-brown, in the latter case more like the leg colour of a Willow Warbler.

The race *exsul*, from Lanzarote, is (or was, since it is now probably extinct) similar to *canariensis* but is deep greenish-olive tinged with brown on the forehead to nape and lighter greenish-olive on the mantle to the rump and edges to the flight feathers and the tail base. The supercilium is pale yellowish-white over light greenish-olive mottled with yellowish speckles on the cheeks and ear-coverts. The underparts are paler or less intensely yellow or mixed with buff on the breast, the flanks are tinged with warm buff, the thighs are as in *canariensis* and the undertail-coverts are pale yellowish-white; the legs are very dark brown or black. It is also noticeably smaller and has shorter wings than the other races. From the skins that I have seen, the differences between the birds of this race and *canariensis* are slight, just a shade or two different in the colour tones of the upperparts – probably insufficient to warrant subspecific separation of *exsul* from its very close neighbour. In any case, the former, which occurred in

A drab and worn looking adult Chiffchaff of the nominate race in southern England in late summer.

one valley of northern Lanzarote, is probably extinct since none has been seen since the 1940s.

The moult patterns of these southern races have been little studied and most of the available information comes from museum skins, which provide us with only a vague or sketchy picture. It seems likely that there is only one moult a year, following the breeding season, when adult and immature birds undergo a complete post-nuptial and post-juvenile moult respectively. In the race(s) resident on the Canary Islands, the absence of a pre-nuptial moult is perhaps more easily understood since preparations for the breeding season do not require a long and stressful journey. Most birds are unlikely to be aged successfully in the field except in the summer or more usually the late summer period when worn adults, prior to their moult, occur alongside the newly (or more recently) fledged juveniles, which are in fresh plumage; following the post-breeding moult, the adults (now also in fresh plumage) are virtually identical to first-year birds.

Another taxonomic complication occurs with the Chiffchaffs that breed in the mountains of northern Anatolia and the central Taurus range in northern and western Turkey. These have been variously classed as belonging to the nominate race *collybita*, which breeds in Thrace, north-west Turkey, and to *abietinus* which breeds in the Caucasus. They have also been treated by Watson (1962) as a separate race, *brevirostris*, as there are apparently differences both structurally and in plumage from *abietinus*, their closest relative. The wings are slightly shorter and the second primary is also proportionately shorter, the upperparts are darker or greyer than *abietinus*, the breast is lightly streaked with lemon-yellow and the breast and flanks are washed with buff. The presence of these birds gives rise to a number of questions or possibilities, all of which require further investigation before we are certain of their true affinities. They may in fact be sufficiently separable from *abietinus* to warrant subspecific classification or, given that there is a clinal variation in *abietinus*, they may differ no more than other populations which are currently embraced within *abietinus*. Also, the presence of the race *lorenzii* of the Mountain Chiffchaff immediately to the east in the extreme north-east of Turkey suggests that the birds within this region, which may even include the isolated population of *abietinus* in the Caucasus, are moving away from each other and are in the process of evolving into species or recognisable races. Only time and a detailed study will reveal the true situation.

It should also be borne in mind that the Chiffchaff, like a large number of other widely dispersed breeding species, is able to produce some abnormal or aberrant plumages. There are records of birds in Europe showing (partly or wholly) albinism, leucism and melanism in the plumage, together with schizochroism – where yellow is the dominant colour. In more extreme and isolated cases, such as an individual in Holland in December 1992, the bill may be extensively pale or yellow, the tertials strongly patterned and the legs and feet orange-yellow to yellow.

Differences from similar species

Willow Warbler

Throughout most of its breeding range (from the Canaries to eastern Siberia) the Chiffchaff occurs alongside the one species it most resembles, the Willow Warbler. To the untrained eye, these two species are extremely similar in size, shape and plumage. It is only in the small details of plumage, structure, behaviour and habitat occupation that the main differences emerge while the song, of course, is diagnositc. In size and

Comparison of the closed wing shape of Chiffchaffs (top) and Willow Warblers. Note the compact and more rounded shape to the primaries of the Chiffchaff.

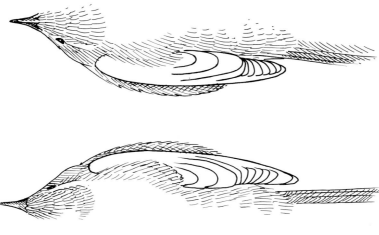

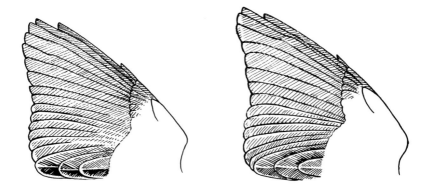

Comparison of the wing shape when spread: the Chiffchaff wing (left) is shorter, more rounded and is emarginated on the 3rd to 6th primaries than that of the Willow Warbler (right).

---

shape the Willow Warbler is slightly larger or longer and looks neater and more attenuated or sleek than the more rounded or dumpy Chiffchaff.

In the hand, it can easily be seen that the Chiffchaff has a fairly short wing (53–68 mm in length from the bend of the wing) made up of bunched or evenly spaced flight feathers. The Willow Warbler's wing is slightly longer (60–70 mm), and has a longer primary projection (i.e. the area of exposed primaries showing beyond the secondaries on the closed wing) caused primarily by a visible gap between the longer second and third primaries. The two species also differ by Chiffchaffs having a shorter second primary and emarginations (see diagram) on the third to the sixth primaries but Willow Warblers have only the third to the fifth primaries emarginated – a subtle difference, but sufficient to take the Willow Warbler as a long-distance migrant to the southern tropics of Africa for the winter.

With experience of both species in the field further subtle differences between the two emerge. One of the most visible is the colour of the legs: bright or pale straw-brown on Willow Warbler dark brown, blackish or jet-black (depending on the race) on Chiffchaff. This rule, however, may not always be considered utterly reliable, since Conder and Keighley (1950) recorded a small percentage of Willow Warblers (probably first-winter birds) with dark slate-coloured legs and Chiffchaffs with rufous to greyish-brown and dark brown legs (or, more aberrantly, yellowish, as given in the instance above). Willow Warbler legs are also slightly thicker than those of the more spindly Chiffchaff. Chiffchaffs also tend to have a more rounded head when compared with the longer, more evenly shaped crown of Willow Warbler and a slightly larger eye than the latter's.

The Willow Warbler is usually a much brighter bird (though there are exceptions, with some individuals being dull brown) with a greater extent of clean or bright yellow in the supercilium and on the underparts. Chiffchaffs, particularly juveniles and birds in autumn and winter, have bright or prominent white eye-crescents (or a broken eye-ring), which are reduced or absent on most Willows. The supercilium on Willows is often quite long and well defined, especially behind the eye, whereas on Chiffchaffs it is more often (particularly on nominate *collybita*) poorly defined. The bill is paler on Willow Warblers, with pale or bright orange extending some way (more visibly) along the base of the lower mandible and on the cutting edges of the upper mandible. With practice, spring adults are fairly easy to separate, as Willows are pale green or pale olive-green on the upperparts and yellowish on the supercilium, whilst Chiffchaffs are duller olive or browner and with dingy buff on the flanks, which generally lack any bright yellow tones.

Mountain Chiffchaff

Occuring in the Caucasus and east to the western Himalayas is the Mountain Chiffchaff, which is very similar in size and shape to the Chiffchaff, particularly those of the race *abietinus*, to which it is clearly related. Until recently the Mountain Chiffchaff was considered as another race of the Chiffchaff, but research undertaken by Voous (1977) and Williamson (1983) showed that, on morphological and geographical grounds, it was best treated as a separate species; some taxonomic authorities, however, disagree with this treatment and it is variably classified elsewhere as a further race (or races) of the Chiffchaff. More recently, it has been proposed by Monroe and Sibley (1993) that the nominate race *sindianus* from the western Himilayas should now be reconsidered as a race of Chiffchaff and that the paler race *lorenzii* be recognized as a new species – the Caucasian Chiffchaff.

Both populations of Mountain Chiffchaff are very similar to *abietinus* Chiffchaffs and lack almost all yellow, green or olive-green in the plumage. The race *lorenzii*, which overlaps with the *abietinus* race of Chiffchaff (although they are separated altitudinally), has the upperparts brownish, occasionally tinged warm brown, and washed with grey. The long, pale or whitish-buff supercilia (which are often joined across the forehead) are well defined and often broadest between the bill and the eye, tapering to a point beyond the end of the ear-coverts, and underlined by a fairly broad dark eye-stripe. The wings and tail feathers are dark brown with fine narrow olive-brown (not greenish) edges; the underwing-coverts vary from white or off-white to cream, more rarely pale yellow. The underparts are off-white, and tinged with buffish-brown or brownish-grey on the breast, flanks, vent and undertail-coverts. The bill is blackish with a dull yellow or pale horn base to the lower mandible and cutting edges of the upper mandible, but this is likely to be seen only at close range.

The nominate eastern race *sindianus* is slightly paler or warmer brown on the upperparts, with a heavier grey tone on the crown, mantle, scapulars and edges to the wing-coverts, the upperparts being noticeably greyer in worn plumage. The flanks are also a warm brown but in worn plumage appear duller or drab brown. The supercilium is as in *lorenzii*, but the paler head lacks the strongly defined eye-stripe. In worn plumage, the upperparts are paler and the underparts are whiter than those of *lorenzii*.

Within both races there is some variation in the colour of the upperparts since some birds of the race *lorenzii* can appear much darker. In fresh plumage, both races, (but mostly *sindianus*, since it is paler or greyer) are very likely to be confused with autumn *abietinus* and *tristis* Chiffchaffs (the latter of which do not occur in the areas occupied by Mountain Chiffchaff), but the lack of any olive-green and the long and well-defined supercilium, relatively pale face and whitish underparts, and again the call which is distinctive, may be the only features on which to base an identification.

Bonelli's Warbler

Confusion also is likely with the Bonelli's Warbler, which breeds in southern Europe and around the Mediterranean and east to Turkey. This is a very pale or plain-looking member of the *Phylloscopus* genus and can be confused with pale autumn (*tristis*) Chiffchaffs. In reality, Bonelli's Warblers are virtually plain-faced with a large eye and have silvery-grey on the upperparts (western birds are slightly more grey-green than the plainer grey or dingy grey eastern race *orientalis*), and are characterized by their bright or lime-green edges to the greater coverts, secondaries, tertials and bases of the outer tail feathers. The face is almost featureless, lacking any eye-stripe and with at best only a faint supercilium; it does, however, show a thin pale buff eye-ring, giving the eye a rather prominent or beady appearance in the centre of an otherwise plain face. In late winter to summer, adults have a pale yellowish-green rump, which on first-winter birds in autumn is duller and less visible. Both ages have well-defined pale green edges to the outer tail feathers. The underparts are almost silvery-white in spring, or washed with buff on eastern birds and autumn adults. The bill is almost entirely pale pinkish, with only the ridge and tip of the upper mandible brown. The legs and feet are dull brown but can be pinkish or slightly greyish-brown, and most show a flesh-pink rear to the legs.

A spring Chiffchaff of the race abietinus. This bird shows a distinctly paler frosting to the plumage.

Radde's and Dusky Warblers

In mid- to late autumn, small numbers of Radde's and Dusky Warblers move or migrate west and south-west (i.e. in the wrong direction) from their breeding grounds east of the Urals across central Asia and occur as vagrants at various headlands, peninsulas or islands in or around the North Sea or, more rarely, elsewhere in northern Europe. In the British Isles, there have been at least 130 records of Radde's Warbler and a little over 100 Dusky Warblers since 1958.

Of the two, Radde's is least likely to be confused with a Chiffchaff since it is a rather chunky, squat-looking warbler with a rounded shape, large or broad head, thick bill, strongly marked face pattern of long, broad supercilium and eye-stripe, olive-green tinged brown upperparts and thick yellowish-brown or straw yellow legs; it often shows dull yellowish-brown undertail-coverts. It skulks, keeping to low undergrowth, where it is most often detected by its short, sharp, clicking 'tuk' or 'tyuk' call note.

Autumn Dusky Warblers are far more likely to cause problems, as many of their features are similar to those shown by dark Chiffchaffs, and it is fine points of plumage and familiarity with the range of plumage variations in Chiffchaffs, particularly those birds in autumn which are clearly not of local origin, that will help separate the two. Dusky is a much darker bird than any brown Chiffchaff. It has deep brown, olive-tinged upperparts, which in some lights can appear tinged with rufous, the rump is slightly paler brown, becoming warmer in tone on the uppertail-coverts. The Dusky also lacks the yellow bend-of-the-wing feather(s) shown by most Chiffchaffs. The supercilium is long, thin and white or whitish, occasionally tinged with buff or brownish-buff over the ear-coverts; it usually begins thinly or finely on the lores, whereas on some Chiffchaffs it is broad over the lores or fine across the base of the forehead. Both Dusky Warbler and Chiffchaff share the broken white eye-ring, but on Dusky this is given some emphasis by the broad dark brown eye-stripe and the mottled white and rust-brown cheeks and ear-coverts. The underparts on Dusky are dull or creamy-white, with a buffish wash or rust-brown tinge to the flanks; similar (or dusky-looking) Chiffchaffs rarely, if ever, show rust-brown flanks. The Dusky Warbler's bill appears dark brown or blackish but has a pinkish or warm yellow base to the lower mandible; eastern Chiffchaffs of the race *abietinus* show a mostly black or blackish bill with only a reduced amount of pink at the base of the lower mandible. As with Radde's Warbler, Dusky Warblers are frequent skulkers in low vegetation and undergrowth, although generally more arboreal and visible than Radde's, and can remain undetected until they give their hard 'tek', 'tack' or 'chek' call note.

Booted Warbler

Mention must also be made of one species outside the *Phylloscopus* group with which confusion is frequently considered likely. This is the Booted Warbler, the smallest member of the larger and for the most part fairly green, grey to grey-green or pale brown *Hippolais* warblers. Booted Warblers are about the same size as a Chiffchaff and have a similar compact but slightly longer-tailed appearance. They have a rounded head, a short and fine bill and fairly short wings, also with a short primary projection. They are remarkably active and agile and frequently flick their wings and tail, particularly when feeding, but rarely dip the tail in the same manner as other (larger) *Hippolais* or Chiffchaffs. Booted Warblers in spring and summer have pale brown upperparts and off-white underparts; a long buffish-white supercilium which often broadens visibly behind the eye and is given some emphasis by the long dark eye-stripe and the faint (but often visible at close range) dark sides to the crown. In autumn plumage the adults are greyer, while the first-winter birds are paler brown, often referred to as the colour of weak or milky tea, on the upperparts, with a rather prominent paler panel made up of the paler brown edges to the secondaries and tertials; another feature, although much less easy to see (more likely in flight), is the off-white or whitish-buff edges to the outer tail feathers. The bill of both adults and first-years is dark brown on the upper mandible and pale pinkish or even yellowish on the lower. The legs of both ages are grey or greyish-horn.

Greenish Warbler

Greenish Warblers are very similar to Chiffchaffs, especially those of the race *tristis* in autumn, when both species are in fresh plumage. Greenish differ mainly in the green or predominantly greenish tones of the upperparts and the extent and colour of the wingbar; the latter is white or yellowish-white (but varies in intensity and can be pale yellow), narrow and well defined, and restricted to the tips of the outer four to six greater coverts, although in the field it will probably appear to be on the tips of all the visible greater coverts. Some Chiffchaffs of the eastern races *abietinus* and *tristis*, particularly the latter, can, in autumn and early winter, show small or short wingbars on the tips of the greater coverts. Wingbars when present on autumn/winter Chiffchaffs tend to be poorly defined and dull or pale grey, buff or buffish-white (rarely white).

The upperparts on Greenish are usually green with a definite greyish tinge or cast. The whitish or yellowish-white supercilium is distinctively long and well defined, usually extending beyond the ear-coverts to the sides of the nape, where it may curve or kink slightly upwards. The cheeks and ear-coverts are pale buffish-white, dull white or mottled with darker bases, and this, together with the long supercilium and well-defined broad eye-stripe, creates a different face pattern. The legs of both Greenish Warbler and Chiffchaff are dark, but on the former they vary and in a good view can be seen to be dark grey or brownish-grey with lighter or yellowish-brown rear of the tarsus and soles of the feet. The upper mandible and tip to the lower is dark, but the rest of the lower mandible is yellowish to pinkish-orange: an important feature in eliminating a possible 'wingbarred' *tristis* Chiffchaff, which has a predominantly black bill.

3

DISTRIBUTION

The world range of the entire genus of *Phylloscopus* warblers encompasses the whole of Europe, Asia and most of Africa, extending from the Canaries in the west to Japan and western Alaska in the east; the northern limits are reached at about 75°N by the most northerly breeding Arctic Warblers, and in the south Willow Warblers spend the winter from the southern limits of the Sahara to the tip of Cape Province, South Africa. The genus has its origins closely tied to the Himalayas, where over 20 species occur, principally from the area of the Hindu Kush and Kashmir to northern Kansu in northern China. This contrasts with the more Mediterranean ancestry of the *Sylvia* family of warblers.

Throughout this vast range the genus can be divided into smaller or more compact geographic units. In the west (taking the Himalayas as the centre of the range), both Wood and Bonelli's Warblers are, for the most part, breeding birds of Europe and North Africa, their ranges overlapped partly by those of the Chiffchaff and Willow Warbler, which occupy not only sizable areas in Europe but also extend their breeding ranges across much of northern Asia. Greenish and Arctic Warblers, have expanded westwards in recent times into Europe and now breed almost continuously from northern and eastern Scandinavia the shores of the Baltic into Asia proper, east of the Urals. In the south-western corner of Asia, Mountain Chiffchaff and Green Warbler are found, while a little further towards central Asia is the range of Plain Leaf Warbler.

As already noted, however, the taxonomic arrangement of the genus is seemingly under constant review, with considerable differences among various taxonomists on what are full species that are true *Phylloscopus* warblers and, having established that, what are races. Currently, Two-barred Greenish and Green Warblers are not recognized as full species in Britain, although they are in the former USSR and elsewhere within their breeding and wintering ranges. Similarly, some taxonomists or national avifaunal authorities recognize some races as full species (e.g. Hume's Yellow-browed Warbler). Another taxonomic complication is the inclusion by some authorities of about six species of African warblers and about eight other species from Indonesia and islands in the western Pacific within the current composition of the genus, which presents a very confused overall picture for the student of species classification and distribution. I prefer to admit only those species which breed within the Palearctic or range just beyond its limits into the Oriental region and winter in this and the Afrotropical region, which gives a more visibly related group of 34 species.

Within the distribution pattern of the whole genus the Chiffchaff is a relatively successful species. It has been able to adapt to diverse habitats

The Chiffchaff's breeding range covers most of Europe and northern central Asia. Note the small outposts in the Canaries and NW Africa. The eastern end of the range is poorly defined and probably lies in the vast forests of eastern Siberia.

and has a very wide distribution encompassing the continental and oceanic boreal, temperate and Mediterranean climatic zones. Its range extends from the isolated outposts in the Canaries and parts of North Africa, north-east through south and central Europe to the Urals in central Russia and the great expanse of forests in central and eastern Siberia. The main geographic boundaries are formed roughly by the 50°F July isotherm in the north, which approximates to 68°-70°N in Norway and Russia, the most northerly points of the range. The southern boundary of the breeding range is the western Canary Isles and almost continuously from Portugal and Spain east through southern Europe to the Balkans and the western and north-western shores of the Black Sea through the Ukraine to southern central USSR and southern Siberia north of 50°N. The easternmost limits are somewhere between the Kolyma and Anadyr rivers in eastern Siberia, but the range is poorly known and may not be beyond the area of Yakutsk on the Lena river. There are isolated populations breeding in the mountains of northern and western Turkey and in the Caucasus and sporadically south and east to the Elburz range in north-west Iran.

The nominate race

The breeding range of the nominate race extends from Ireland in the north-west eastwards through Wales, England and central and southern

Scotland (occasionally further north) to Denmark, with a small isolated outpost, most probably of this race, now established in Skåne in southern Sweden; also south through most of west and southern and central Germany to southern Poland. It occurs throughout France and most of northern and central Europe east to Romania, and through the central and western mountain ranges of Italy and the highlands of north-east Sicily. The southern border of the range is formed by the Pyrenees, where it intergrades with the race *brehmii* in the small area of overlap in extreme south-west France. In south-east Europe it occurs throughout Bulgaria, the former area of Yugoslavia and into extreme northern Greece and Thrace in north-west Turkey, where it just reaches the Bosphorus.

In winter the population moves west and south and, depending on the severity of the winter, occurs sporadically (and usually in the more sheltered areas) in south-west Ireland and, perhaps more regularly, in south-west England, with occasional mid-winter records also from sheltered areas in most of central and southern England, south Wales and more rarely north to southern Scotland. On the mainland of Europe it winters in the western part of the Netherlands, again sparingly and not in any great number, and west and southwards through France. As in southern England, it becomes more numerous or regular as a wintering bird in the more sheltered or warmer maritime provinces of the western seaboard, from Brittany south along to the northern flanks of the Pyrenees.

The main wintering area is from southern central France, although it appears to avoid the Massif Central, and around the Mediterranean from Spain and Portugal to Italy, Greece, western and southern Turkey and

A Chiffchaff of the race abietinus or tristis in autumn showing pale tips and edges to some of the wing feathers. In the field, the pale tips to the greater coverts look like a wingbar.

most of the Mediterranean islands. In the Middle East, the wintering range continues south through Lebanon, Syria, the extreme west of Jordan and Israel through the Sinai desert and into northern Egypt, where it occurs throughout the Nile delta. It also winters down the Nile to central Sudan (slightly south of Khartoum) and into the highlands of northern Ethiopia. Elsewhere, in central and western North Africa, *collybita* winters in northern and central Morocco, northern Algeria, northern and central Tunisia and (usually in small numbers) at many of the desert oases in the northern and central Sahara, west to coastal Mauretania. On the Canary Islands, small numbers winter mainly on the eastern islands of Fuerteventura and Lanzarote, with fewer on Gran Canaria and Tenerife. On the southern edge of the Sahara it is a common winter visitor in the Gambia, Senegal and along the banks of the Niger in Mali and southern Niger, south to about 12°S, where it mingles with Chiffchaffs of the race *abietinus* from further north and east. According to B. Lamarche (1981), a considerable number remain in Mali during the northern summer.

Distribution in the British Isles

The recent history of the Chiffchaff in the British Isles is dependent upon the availability of deciduous woodland. At some time between 6000 and 8000 years ago, extensive areas of deciduous woods built up in Britain following the end of glaciation. At this time there must have been large areas where the Chiffchaff was able to find ideal nesting habitats. The first documented record appears in the literature of Willughby and Ray in 1678 (although, of course, at that stage it was not known as the Chiffchaff). According to Colin Harrison, however, in his *History of the Birds of Britain* bones of either a Chiffchaff or a Willow Warbler, recovered from Derbyshire, probably date from the latter part of the last glaciation (about ten thousand years ago). Harrison goes on to speculate that it was probably less common or widespread at that time, when most of the ancient woodland was at its climax stage and the canopy closed out the necessary undergrowth. The bird was able to breed in glades, clearings or along the edges of the great woods. Following this period, with the increase in the human population and the clearance of much of the woodlands of central and lowland Britain, the Chiffchaff must have enjoyed a considerable renaissance and numbers probably increased over a prolonged period. This growth was allowed to continue only until the destruction of their woodland habitat became too extensive and man started removing, at an increasing rate, much of the prime areas of breeding habitat.

In more recent periods of recorded ornithological time, the distribution of the Chiffchaff in Britain has been fairly constant and consistent with the spread of suitable woods and copses, these becoming abundant in some places. During most of the present century the population has shown a slow and gradual increase, with several short-term checks or declines (either on a local or, more worryingly, a national basis) in the trend, particularly in the more recent decades. Within Britain, the Chiffchaff is commonest in the southern half, south of a line from the Mersey to the

Humber. This is not to say, however, that this area contains the most densely populated part of the range, since some of the areas of prime or optimal habitat in northern England and south-west Scotland may be as densely occupied as anywhere in southern England or Wales.

In England, the highest densities are found in the south-western counties from Gloucestershire and Hereford and Worcestershire south to Cornwall and east through most of the southern counties to Sussex and parts of Kent. The evidence available indicates that the Chiffchaff has only recently, since the early years of this century, begun to breed on the Isle of Man. Ralfe, writing in 1905, gave records of singing birds in the springs of 1874 and 1882. The first BTO Atlas recorded breeding in at least seven 10 km squares and by the second, for the years 1998-91, breeding was recorded in six 10 km squares.

The distribution of the bird in Wales is clearly linked to the areas of favoured habitat, tracts of mature woodlands with a good covering or well-developed layer of plants such as nettles, ferns or brambles. It is therefore surprising that the recent breeding-bird surveys of the British Isles found that the Chiffchaff is not nearly so plentiful or abundant as it might be in an area of Britain known chiefly for its wealth of widespread deciduous woodlands. Further investigation by Roger Lovegrove et al. (1994) found that overgrazing by sheep, especially on the upland or hillside woods, has deprived many of the suitable woodlands of the essential ground cover required by the Chiffchaff for breeding.

Despite this, the bird remains common, particularly in the woods of the south and south-east and in one or two other less degraded areas; a glance at the breeding-distribution map shows that it breeds, or has recently bred, in about 90-95 per cent of the 10 km squares in Wales. It is absent only from the mountainous areas of the central and north, although it is present even on the lower slopes of the Snowdon range, where, in instances recalling habitat utilization by birds in northern Scotland, it has taken to nesting in woodlands with an understorey of rhododrendrons.

Most of the Scottish population breeds in the central lowlands and southern Borders, with a small incursion northwards along the sheltered woods of the west coast and up through the Great Glen to the area around Inverness. The area of greatest abundance is the south-west from Dumfries and Galloway and the Borders north to Argyll; it is notably common in roadside plantations around Glasgow and seems fairly well represented in the woods around Loch Lomond.

In northern Scotland, in the area to the north and west of the Great Glen, Chiffchaffs nest on a fairly regular basis, but, while they are not common and numbers may vary greatly from year to year, nesting may be more regular than is currently recorded. There has clearly been an extension of the range northwards in the last forty years, as Baxter and Rintoul (1953) knew of no confirmed breeding north of Oban. Chiffchaffs now breed, or have bred, in every mainland county of north Scotland, even as far north as the north coast, and have occasionally ventured west to breed on the islands of Rhum, Mull, Eigg, Skye and Raasay. Valerie Thom (1986) stated that there was then no confirmation of birds breeding on the

Outer Hebrides, but since the mid 1980s, up to two pairs have bred annually in the sparse woods on the Uists. It is easy to speculate that the number of birds reaching or remaining in Scotland to breed is entirely linked to the prevailing weather pattern of the middle and late spring, and it seems quite probable that in years with mild early springs more birds push further north than in years with cold or late springs.

The earlier BTO Atlas covering the years 1968–72 recorded the Chiffchaff as having probably bred in Orkney, but this was not confirmed and, although it was strongly suspected on Rousay in 1977, by the time of the publication of the second Atlas for the years 1988–91 the situation remained unchanged. There has seemingly been an increase in the number of singing birds apparently occupying territory late in the spring in suitable breeding areas in northern Scotland, including many of the Inner and Outer Hebrides north to Lewis, where Chiffchaffs regularly sing until late in the spring or early summer. A single bird sang, on the remote island of St Kilda from the beginning of April to early June 1965 but failed to attract a mate to this most unlikely of breeding sites.

In Ireland, there has been a noticeable increase in the Chiffchaff's range during the present century. In the latter years of the nineteenth century the bird was present in only seven widely separated counties, but since then the range has expanded and it has bred in every county, although it must be added that numbers of breeding birds are extremely small in some areas, particularly northern Mayo and Donegal, where in some years there may be none at all. Only in parts of south-west Ireland does it become as common as the Willow Warbler.

Chiffchaffs now breed regularly in almost every county of Ireland and are only absent from one or two small areas such as north-west Mayo, south-west Galway and the peninsulas of Kerry. The distribution is mainly central and southern, with highest densities found in the counties of Cork, Meath, Cavan, Fermanagh and Tyrone, while the woods of Kilkenny in the south-east also support a sizable part of the population.

Although not generally recognized as part of the British Isles geographically, the Channel Islands have been extensively surveyed as part of both BTO breeding-bird Atlases. Much of the habitat on the Islands is extremely suitable for the Chiffchaff and it is a common breeding bird. Although there are breeding records for the main islands of Guernsey and Jersey dating from the end of the previous century, the surveys for the two Atlases show that there has been a slight increase in numbers and area between the years 1968–72 and 1988–91.

Distribution of the races – *abietinus*

The Chiffchaffs breeding in central and eastern Germany and central and northern Poland are probably intermediates between *collybita* and *abietinus*. Most of the range of *abietinus* lies to the east of Europe and extends from eastern Germany (Prussia) through northern Poland and the Baltic States;

Two races of the Chiffchaff and the Willow Warbler.

P.c. collybita
1st winter

P.c. collybita adult
autumn/winter

P.c. collybita
Juvenile

P.c. collybita
adult winter

Willow Warbler
1st winter

P.c. albietinus
1st winter

Willow Warbler adult

in Scandinavia it breeds through much of the coastal regions of Norway, and in southern Sweden extending north mainly in coastal regions to about 67°N and continuing east into Finland across the southern borders of Lapland. At the extreme northern edge of the range it is a common passage migrant to the Faroes and in 1981 one pair bred at Torshavn. This race also breeds in the southern part of the Kola Peninsula and around the shores of the White Sea east to the Pechora river and south through the central Urals to the region of Odessa on the Black Sea, but is absent from the rest of southern Ukraine and western and southern Kazakhstan. In the south there is an isolated population which occurs through the Caucasus into Armenia and along the highlands of the Black Sea coastlands in northern Turkey, and in northern Iran it extends eastwards to south-east of the Caspian Sea along the Elburz range (to slightly east of Tehran).

In autumn, *abietinus* moves south or south-west to winter sporadically in south-east Romania, and continuously through Macedonia, Greece and Thrace, the western and southern coastal areas of Turkey, Cyprus and through the countries bordering the eastern Mediterranean, being found in quite high numbers alongside nominate *collybita* in the pine forests of northern and central Israel, and in the desert oases and along the edges of cultivation south to southern Iraq, occuring more thinly and more sporadically to western Iran. It winters more numerously in Saudi Arabia and Kuwait, Oman, North and South Yemen and across the Red Sea to most of Ethiopia (where it occurs with individuals of the nominate race) and southern Sudan (mainly in the highlands above 1800 m) and occasionally or rarely to southern Egypt. It is also a winter visitor to the highlands of northern Somalia, and is present from December to April in the central highlands of Kenya (usually between 2200 and 3700 m) within the 1000 mm rainfall zone and the Mau forest and at lower levels (down to 1400 m) in northern Kenya. The southern boundary is reached in northern Tanzania (Mt Kilimanjaro). Records in the neighbouring areas of western Kenya and eastern Uganda are of birds on passage earlier in the winter or in early spring. Many individuals either make a diagonal crossing of the Sahara or migrate along its southern flank, since at least half the wintering population of Chiffchaffs in Senegal (and possibly many of those in Mali and Niger) are of this race.

The race *tristis*

East of *abietinus* lies the range of the race *tristis*; this has a poorly defined area of overlap with that of *abietinus* (see note on '*fulvescens*' in Chapter 2), as many birds are indeterminate between the two races. Most birds that are recognizable as true *tristis* occur in western Siberia, east of the Pechora river and middle Urals north to the tree-limit at about 71°N across Siberia to the Lena river and probably discontinuously further east to the Kolyma River or even the Anadyr, but confirmation that the range is continuous is lacking. In the south, it ranges eastwards through northern Kazakhstan to the mountains of the central Altai and the western Sayan ranges to the source area of the Lena, the mountains of the Tannu Ola, and through the extensive forests on the western shore of Lake Baikal. It may also possibly extend (occasionally or regularly in more recent years) to north-west Mongolia, but according to Kozlova (1933) most records from there involve birds on spring and autumn passage.

While some (probably only a very few) individuals of this race winter in Uzbekistan and southern Turkmenistan, most move south to winter south of the breeding range in southern Iran (possibly also southern or south-east Iraq) and east through Baluchistan, Pakistan and northern India (south to northern Maharashtra) to Sikkim, Bhutan and Bangladesh. A few also winter in the foothills of the Himalayas in southern Nepal.

The race *brehmii*

Chiffchaffs of the race *brehmii* are found in the extreme south-west of France (mainly Aquitaine and the foothills of the northern Pyrenees), the northern and central areas of Spain and most of Portugal. In the west it reaches the south of Portugal and the mountains of Cadiz, in the northern and central areas of Spain it breeds in the northern Meseta along river courses and to a lesser extent in the valleys of southern Spain, but in most of the south and east it is absent with only breeding outposts in the higher areas of southern Murcia and Andalucia and around Gibraltar. It is, in general, rather sparsely distributed, with breeding densities much lower than those of nominate and *abietinus* birds. Although occuring at fairly high elevation, it is not among the highest-breeding birds, scarcely going above 1200 m but reaching the upper tree-limit in the eastern Pyrenees.

Recent evidence from Segovia suggests that some of the birds breeding in that area may be of the nominate race *collybita*, since their song is not of the typical *brehmii* types. This has led to some uncertainty about the status of the two races in Spain. Several authors have commented on the possible unreliability of song as a feature separating *brehmii* from other races. This has also been supported by the trapping of a bird in Belgium which was giving the song of *brehmii* yet had the wing formula of the nominate race.

In North Africa, *brehmii* breeds in isolated outposts in extreme northern Morocco and east of there into the Atlas mountains of northern Algeria and the oak forests in northern Tunisia. In late autumn it makes short-distance movements to lower altitudes and the population generally spreads out within Spain and Portugal, with many wintering in the parks of Madrid and the coastal lowlands, particularly in the south and south-east, where it is frequently recorded in suburban gardens. Movements are generally as far south as central Morocco and Algeria, where it occurs with birds of the nominate race.

The races *canariensis* and *exsul*

Of the remaining races, *canariensis* and *exsul* are entirely sedentary. The former occupies the islands of the western Canaries from La Palma and Hierro to Gran Canaria, while *exsul* (a doubtful race and probably now extinct) was resident in Haria Valley on Lanzarote in the eastern Canaries.

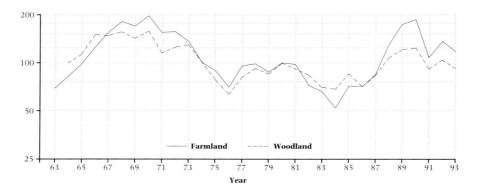

Chiffchaff population and trends taken from the BTO Common Birds Census index.

Population and trends

In the British Isles the present distribution and presumably the overall numbers of breeding pairs are slowly increasing, but the species is not so common or widespread as its near relative the Willow Warbler, which nationally outnumbers the Chiffchaff by about four to one. Although many of the suitable woodlands and forests of England and Wales are inhabited by breeding pairs, there are a number of gaps in its distinction. The valleys of the central uplands of the Pennines to the Border hills, parts of central and northern Wales and the lowlands of the East Anglian fens remain as notable blank spots on both the national breeding-bird Atlases of 1968-72 and 1989-91 (in many of these areas the woods and copses are heavily grazed by sheep, and there may be no understorey vegetation.

The trend in the British breeding population of Chiffchaffs is reflected in the surveys undertaken by the BTO, notably the Common Bird Census (CBC), which indicates the status of common breeding birds in Britain since 1962. The CBC is an index of relative population values for each year based on reports from a sample of woodland or farmland habitats in Britain. Most of these sites are in England but do, nevertheless, give a fair representation of national trends. The CBC index for Chiffchaff shows that the population declined in the 1970s and has been slightly variable or fluctuating since then, but the overall trend, as we have seen reflected in the distribution in Scotland, is one of increase.

Once these trends have been identified and confirmed over a number of years, it is possible to analyse their causes. In the case of the Chiffchaff, as with a number of other summer migrants to Europe, a pattern emerged that matched changes in weather patterns in the Mediterranean region and the amount of rainfall in the Sahel district along the southern edge of the Sahara. It is in this area that an unknown number of *collybita* and *abietinus* Chiffchaffs spend the winter. The rainfall in the Sahel declined rapidly during the early to middle 1970s and showed only a partial recovery towards the end of the decade, only to fall back sharply to drought proportions in 1984. Since then, a period of amelioration in the rains has brought about the recent improvement in the fortunes of the Chiffchaff population and those of other species such as Sand Martin, Blackcap, Sedge Warbler and Spotted Flycatcher, whose main wintering areas or refuelling sites lie within the Sahel and for which the annual amount of rainfall is crucial to their survival and that of the habitat on which they depend.

While the drought in the Sahel is one of the decisive factors affecting numbers of migrants returning to breed in Europe, the pattern of dramatic population crash of previously common to abundant species has not been quite so marked or prominent in the Chiffchaff as it has been for some species such as Whitethroat, Sedge Warbler or Redstart. That Chiffchaffs are not so severely affected as these species is partly due to the fact that only some of the population migrates to the south of the Sahara for the winter, and the continued viability of the wintering areas north of the Sahara, mostly in the countries around the Mediterranean, has served as an effective buffer.

While it is clear that the Chiffchaff is still common and widespread within most of its area, and that there is an abundance of prime or suitable breeding habitat, it should not be taken as guaranteed that this will always be so. We know too little of European and Asiatic weather patterns and temperature shifts to be able to predict long-term trends successfully, let alone the more dynamic and undoubtedly potentially disastrous effects of long-term droughts on the southern borders of the Sahara. Drought and rapid southward expansion of the Sahara in the region of the Sahel possibly represent the most serious threats to the species' present numbers.

A Chiffchaff of the paler 'Siberian' race tristis in Finland in late summer. Small numbers of this race pass through or occasionally winter in Britain.

39

4

WINTERING CHIFFCHAFFS IN BRITAIN

In the early years of the the 19th century several ornithologists, principally Montagu, writing in 1813, came to the conclusion that perhaps not all Chiffchaffs 'quit these shores in winter'. This was based largely on the number of sporadic sightings and records of individual birds seen occasionally in winter when it had, by then, become generally accepted that most of these small warblers flew south for the winter. As the years passed and more winter records were made known from a wider area, extending from southern England to south Wales and southern Ireland, it became clear that a small part of the population stayed north of the main wintering range. These birds winter in sheltered areas such as thick hedgerows, thornscrub or reedbeds, where the micro-climate offers a degree of protection against freezing night temperatures. Clearly their survival depends greatly on the intensity of the northern winter, not only in terms of the numbers remaining but also with regard to their ability to find sufficient food and adequate shelter.

The main wintering range (see Chapter 3) is at least 800 km further south, and even at the northern fringes of this area numbers of birds are not high, so it seems fairly clear that the determining factor is the temperature, which sustains the birds and their insect prey. Since most British winters contain at least one spell of frosty weather, it is reasonable to ask why they remain with us. Maybe it gives those birds wintering to the north of the majority of the population a head start in the rush for breeding areas the following spring.

The BTO Winter Atlas showed that the main wintering area lies south of a line from Flamborough Head to Anglesey, although, perhaps more surprisingly in view of the frequently cold northerly winds and greater chance of severe weather, there are a number of records of Chiffchaffs regularly wintering along the east coast north to Edinburgh and at one or two sites in the lowlands of central Scotland. Even more surprising, perhaps, is the fact that there are, or have been, fairly regular records of wintering birds in Aberdeen, Orkney, Shetland and the Western Isles.

In Devon and Cornwall, Chiffchaffs were first suspected of wintering in 1806 and 1807. Several writers mentioned their presence in winter over the intervening years, but it was not until the winter of 1940/41 that very high numbers were reported. From 20 to 25 December 1940, 50 or more were seen in the area of Falmouth, although this may have been exceptional for such a relatively small area, as there had been severe frosts in Cornwall just prior to these dates which may have forced the birds out of their normal wintering areas. Following this there is little more information to suggest any changes in the numbers of wintering birds until 1972, when an incomplete survey found at least 25 individuals wintering in Cornwall. Since then, R. D. Penhallurick (1978) discovered in the 1970s that sewage farms were a favoured wintering location, and in a survey in the south-west of the county in the winter of 1976/77 he found just over a hundred individuals, most of which were at just eleven sites.

Most of the south-coast counties of Ireland, Wales and England regularly, if not annually, support small numbers in winter, these are usually of single individuals (and certainly no more than three or four) at each site. There are, however, a number of favoured localities in southern and south-central England, again showing a bias towards water, where Chiffchaffs are known to concentrate in slightly higher numbers. There have been winter 'highs' of nine in Northumberland in 1980/81 (which for such a northern coastal county is particularly noteworthy) and 25 in Buckinghamshire in 1982/83. There were in excess of 100 birds in Hampshire in the winters of 1982/83 and 1984/85, numbers reducing to about half that total in the years immediately following this period, but increasing again to over 80 in the winter of 1990/91.

Throughout most of the counties in southern England occasional Chiffchaffs can be found in favoured or sheltered spots, particularly where the conditions are good for feeding, although there are only a few counties, such as those in the south-west, where birds regularly winter at up to ten (or more) sites. It is, however, by no means certain that each site will hold Chiffchaffs, either regularly or throughout the entire winter. Very few of the inland counties, where the reduced effects of the sea could mean the possibility of suffering a prolonged cold spell, match costal areas in either the number of wintering sites or numbers of individuals wintering.

There is, however, a major (and possibly the sole) exception to the rule that inland areas support much smaller numbers than coastal locations, and that is the area of London and its widespread sprawl of suburbs. In the early 1990s, the area around the capital supported up to 54 individuals in the mid-winter months of January and February at just over 30 sites, including two or three sites in the heart of London itself. M. K. Dennis (1993) analysed the numbers and distribution of Chiffchaffs wintering within the area of the capital and found that, combining records for late November and December the population was probably in excess of 60 and in certain winters possibly nearer 100 individuals.

Most Welsh records are from the southern coastal counties but not exclusively so, as the county bird reports show that up to 14 wintered on Anglesey in the winters between 1985 and 1989, 16 in Clwyd between 1976 and 1989 and 27 in Gwynedd between 1985 and 1991, compared with southern county totals of 90 in Pembroke between 1981 and 1990, 44 in Gwent in the same period and up to 168 in Glamorgan between 1980 and 1989. Whether these totals are exceptional or are the result of more Chiffchaffs wintering in recent years or more observers reporting wintering birds is difficult to say, but previous totals for Glamorgan have not only the highest number of wintering Chiffchaffs but also possibly the highest density of birdwatchers in the whole of Wales.

The same pattern of winter presence predominating along the south coast is repeated in Ireland, with most records in the three counties of Cork, Waterford and Wexford, with sporadic winter records from a further 16 counties as far north as Antrim, Donegal and Londonderry. Numbers in Ireland have never been high, perhaps no more than 150 individuals in a good or mild winter. An indication that some of the birds wintering are of relatively local origin is provided by a single ringing recovery: one retrapped at the end of November 1974 had previously been ringed in the breeding season in Londonderry.

Numbers of Chiffchaffs wintering in Scotland have always been much lower than elsewhere, largely because there is less shelter and a much lower average temperature than in areas further south. The BTO Winter Atlas shows most of the records to be in the central lowlands, but with a scattering of records north and west from Aberdeen to around Inverness and, as noted already, at two or three sites on the Northern Isles and occasional occurrences on the Western Isles and at other isolated sheltered spots down the west coast, including the rhododendron woods of Islay.

It has been estimated by the BTO in their Atlas of wintering birds, published in 1986, that in an average year there are probably up to 500 individual Chiffchaffs wintering in Britain and Ireland, and in some winters, particularly the mild ones, probably in excess of 1000 (these figures are, of course, of known individuals; the true numbers may well be up to several times greater. Evidence from ringing at sites which hold wintering Chiffchaffs has shown that there are more present than observations may indicate. For instance, in Hampshire, Clark and Eyre (1993) reported a population of up to eight or so birds at one sewage farm, but ringing operations at the site produced a total of at least 26 between the middle of November and the end of December. Most birds are found in generally sheltered areas, often near water, and while some are able to spend the winter in one locality, others may undertake short movements when sources of food become scarce.

An analysis of the records for southern England shows that most Chiffchaffs first appear at the wintering site in the middle or at the end of November, suggesting a late or delayed passage. Peak numbers at most sites are in late December and early January, and then decline slightly (as birds wander) until the first returning migrants arrive from farther south in early March. This pattern is broken only by the sudden onset of severe weather, which may force the birds to move on, to endure the worst of the weather, or, perhaps the more likely outcome is that the bird succumbs to the weather and the inability to feed. Penhallurick (1978) noted that Chiffchaffs wintering in Cornwall, mostly at sewage farms, began to disperse from the sites by the middle of January, although there was no apparent need to do so as the weather remained favourable throughout. In addition to regular wintering in Britain, there are also a few instances where ringed birds have returned to the same site in successive winters.

42

The numbers of Chiffchaffs wintering in Britain have clearly increased in the last thirty years, and this is documented in many of the annual county bird reports. In the London area, this increase has been particularly noticeable. Mike Dennis (1993) records that prior to 1955 there were just three mid-winter records. In the years immediately following there was a slight but regular increase, with up to 11 birds present in the winter of 1960/61, but smaller numbers in the ensuing years. In the late 1960s, there was a succession of mild winters was accompanied by a corresponding increase in the numbers of Chiffchaffs, wintering to between ten and 20 by the mid 1970s and up to approximately 60 or more by the middle of the 1980s.

This growth over the last three decades has been matched by an increase in the numbers of Blackcaps also wintering in Britain. Although in the early years of this century most of these were, as with the Chiffchaffs, initially in south-west England, since then they have spread to virtually the whole of England, through southern and central Wales, southern and eastern Ireland and the central lowlands of Scotland, and more thinly northwards along the east coast to around Inverness and sporadically to Orkney. The reasons for this sudden increase are not clear. It could, of course, be linked to the run of relatively mild winters, but even more perplexing is the fact that in severe winters, such as that of 1981/82, more Blackcaps were recorded (although in the latter case it may simply be that the birds were more visible to birdwatchers).

Ringing results show that the Blackcaps wintering in Britain are from breeding areas in southern Germany and Austria; there are no records at all of Blackcaps breeding in Britain being recovered here in winter. It also seems that winters with high numbers present follow periods of heavy passage down the east coast in autumn. One of the main differences between wintering Chiffchaffs and Blackcaps is that the latter have no problem in changing their diet from insects throughout the summer to berries and fruit in the autumn and winter.

Although many of the Chiffchaffs wintering in Britain, perhaps the majority at most sites, are of the nominate race, they are joined by others from Scandinavia and further east. These birds, mostly *abietinus* and an even smaller number of *tristis*-type birds, are late-autumn migrants along the east coast of Scotland and both the west and east coasts of England, and part of this passage movement remains to spend the winter in Britain. It was estimated by Cramp *et al.* (1993) that about 40 per cent of the Chiffchaffs wintering in Britain are of one of the eastern races, and Dennis found that 55 per cent of those wintering in Essex were of the northern races. Williamson (1954) examined the weather patterns and the possible areas of origin of the birds on late or delayed passage which may lead to some wintering in Britain. Evidence gained from the patterns of arrival and the associated weather patterns over the northern North Sea, Scandinavia and Russia east of the Urals led him to believe that their area of origin was eastern central Finland and the north-western part of Russia. Clearly, some, if not all, of the birds had travelled some distance to arrive at this point of departure, since the range of the *tristis*-type birds lies well to the east.

5

HABITAT

As a summer home, the Chiffchaff requires fairly old, mature, or at least well-established woods with a good covering of ground flora in which to nest, a range of trees or shrubs that provide sufficient insect food, and weather and temperature conditions that are neither too hot nor too wet. While these requirements may seem to be fairly general, they are, on closer inspection, almost specific to the Chiffchaff.

A few other Palearctic breeding species could be said to have the same requirements, and in this context it would be easy to suggest that the Chaffinch, Willow, Wood and Garden Warblers together with Blackcap and Redstart share the same habitat preference as the Chiffchaff. In each case, however, they have specific demands within the habitat that differ from those of the Chiffchaff. The Chaffinch, for example, differs from the Chiffchaff mainly in that it is not tied to woods of a certain age or structure, it is not limited to a range of insect prey even though most nestlings are fed insect food for their first few days of life, and, perhaps most importantly, it has a greater choice of nesting sites since it does not nest on the ground.

The habitat requirements of the Willow Warbler are perhaps the closest to those of the Chiffchaff. It requires woods of a certain age and structure, foraging and feeding areas similar to those of the Chiffchaff, and a similar amount of ground cover in which to build the nest. Within the parameters of these requirements, however, are a number of factors which separate it from the Chiffchaff. While some woods in Britain may hold both species, the Willow Warbler is more likely to be found in areas of lower vegetation and hence younger woods or plantations, parkland and, most noticeable of all, in scrub. As it is able to utilize a lower growth of vegetation as a breeding site, it is able to breed much further north, into the dwarf juniper and birch forests on the edge of the tundra, than the Chiffchaff does.

Many of the beech or oak woods of the southern and central parts of the Chiffchaff's range are likely to be occupied also by another close relative, the Wood Warbler. In this case, however, there is very little likelihood of competition for territory or nesting sites, since Wood Warblers prefer much less undergrowth than the Chiffchaff, in some cases none at all, and are quite at home with a light scattering of dead leaves, moss and occasional ferns and may tolerate some brambles. When the vegetation becomes too dense or intrusive, (and more to the liking of the Chiffchaff), the Wood Warbler will leave for more open areas.

The breeding habitat of the Chiffchaff is largely characterized as light broadleaved, mixed or coniferous woodland with a loose to moderate scattering of undergrowth; put simply, this is a combination of trees usually at least 5 m tall from which to sing and some kind of an undergrowth layer in which to nest. Within this type of habitat requirement there is a multitude of varying types or stages of woodland in which the bird is able to find food, build a nest and rear its young. These habitat preferences can best be summed up, certainly for nominate and *abietinus* Chiffchaffs, in the following:

1 Variable levels of young to fairly established or mature trees with an open or broken canopy to allow sunlight to penetrate to the floor.
2 The ground or scrub layer of vegetation should be open yet well developed, even if only sparsely distributed within the wood.
3 Ground or scrub layer consisting of poor to medium growth of grasses, herbs, bracken, brambles or nettles.
4 Nest site to be shaded (at least for part of the day) and dry; in moist or damp woods nesting areas are likely to be only in the higher or groundwater-free areas.
5 In closed woods requires a presence of glades, rides or vegetated edge.
6 In cemeteries similar requirements to above, but will accept a good ground or scrub layer with the provision of tall trees (even lone trees).

Within the British Isles such a range of habitats is fairly plentiful, and there is a widespread usage of both the larger areas of woods and forests and comparatively smaller areas of coppiced woods and copses on commons and heaths, in parks and in old or well-established hedgerows (with trees) and some of the more mature (and mixed-species) forestry plantations. It even breeds (but has only recently done so) in areas where such habitat is extremely limited, such as on Lundy and the Isles of Scilly. In much of lowland Britain woods of sufficient size, age and structure are at a premium, so that many are easily taken up with breeding pairs of Chiffchaffs quite early in the spring, particularly in years when the species' density is at a peak. In such years birds may be forced out into what is regarded as overflow or suboptimal habitat, such as linear hedgerows with tall trees and a good shrub layer; studies have shown that in these situations occupation will begin (or be at greatest density) with those territories closest to adjacent woods, with the late arrivers or less competitive individuals furthest away.

In a study of Chiffchaffs breeding in the small scattered woodlands of the Dale peninsula in Pembrokeshire, D. G. Herald and I. A. Johnson (1968) found that the first birds arriving back in the breeding areas rapidly set up territories in the deciduous woodlands and hedgerows, mostly of oak and sycamore, late arrivals taking up residence in the clearly less preferred windblown bushy area, which was only up to 4 m in height. In the latter the birds sang from a row of telegraph poles that ran through the area, but they were, according to the researchers, scruffier and smaller than usual, suggesting that the area was colonized by younger birds unable to establish territories elsewhere.

Throughout the range of *collybita*, *abietinus* and to a certain extent *brehmii* and *tristis* the breeding habitat is much the same. There are, it is

Typical breeding habitat of Chiffchaffs in southern England. A variety of habitats offer shelter and feeding and nesting places.

true, minor variations in the conditions imposed by the changes in and the natural composition of the species of trees, bushes and shrubs that make up the habitat and in the natural forces of climate and temperature that maintain or shape the habitat. Within this range of habitat preferences and occupation, the Chiffchaff as a species, is perhaps entirely successful and is clearly able to sustain the wide spread of its population. There are only slight variations, mainly in height and usually determined by local factors, mostly associated with predators or perhaps lack of suitable habitat in the immediate area of the individual (or pair). Overall it shows little sign of being able to adapt to a wider area of habitat occupation, which is perhaps not so true of the Willow Warbler, which shows a greater level of flexibility in its range of habitat choice. There are, however, one or two isolated instances which suggest that on occasions Chiffchaffs can tolerate less than ideal situations. In June 1953 W. B. Yapp (in Penhallurick) recorded a singing male in dense gorse and blackthorn scrub only 75 cm high on the cliffs at Polperro, Cornwall. In May 1955 several others were heard singing from the coastal scrub along the clifftops of north Cornwall without a tree in sight. More recently R. D. Penhallurick, also referring to Cornwall, records that in June 1977 he watched a family party with recently fledged young in similar scrub on Dodman Point. Elsewhere in Europe, breeding Chiffchaffs have been recorded in such places as industrial wastelands, factory grounds and mine-working areas provided there is a presence of trees and bushes; in the latter case the birds bred on a planted slag-heap.

Throughout much of Europe and western Asia this is a bird of mature lowland woods such as coppiced woods, copses or groves and old or well-established hedgerows or shelterbelts with a fairly well-mixed grouping of

46

medium to tall trees which allow an open canopy and daylight penetration to the floor (for at least part of the year and certainly well into the spring) so that a good growth of medium to tall plants and shrubs is able to thrive. In parts of the range it occurs as a breeding bird in parks and large, old or neglected gardens with deciduous trees and untended areas with a herbaceous ground layer. In areas where it occurs in more closed forest or densely packed woods, such as the sessile oak woods of western Britain and Ireland, and in mixed woods of beech, ash and birch, it more usually breeds at the edges of the wood, where the ground layer of vegetation remains, and can also be found in glades or along forest roads or rides. Such woods provide an abundant area for breeding in the pioneer stage when the wood is comparatively open, but as the growth reaches its climax stage the canopy closes and the ground layer is excluded or manages to exist only at the edges where the daylight penetrates. In other areas Chiffchaffs breed in plantations of broadleaved trees and conifers, from the sapling stage (providing there are trees of some height or maturity present) to more mature stands. They also occur in semi-scrub habitat where there is a progression in age or height of trees such as ash or hawthorn followed by elder or wayfarer, which, in time, will also become more dominant over the remaining scrub.

In parts of the range, particularly the Alps, the Carpathians and the higher areas of Asia, the Chiffchaff is a breeding bird of higher altitudes, including the montane oak and conifer woods and forests in both southern

Woodland edges or glades are a typical habitat used by Chiffchaffs for foraging and nesting.

and eastern Europe and east through the Carpathians, Caucasus, Urals, the central ranges of the Altai and the western Sayan range. There are records of pairs holding territories at up to about 1800 m in the Alps and up to 2150 m in the eastern Pyrenees. In the Carpathians, Dementiev and Gladkov (1951-54) state that *collybita* occurs from the foothills to about 1600 m, where it occurs in the elfin forests at the tree-line; in addition, they state that *abietinus* occurs in summer at up to 2000 m (presumably in the middle Urals and Caucasus) and possibly higher in the upper forest at the boundaries of alpine meadows. Birds breeding in the mature forests of northern Turkey ('*brevirostris*') are not found in summer below 2000 m.

Throughout much of the range of *collybita* and *abietinus* it particularly favours deciduous trees such as beech, oak, alder and willow, although with eastward progression through the range the preference changes towards a more coniferous selection, with spruce, silver fir and pine trees becoming the more normal type of habitat occupied. Although not primarily a bird of conifers in Britain and elsewhere in central Europe, it does show some preference for the more widely spaced areas of larch woods, but within the British Isles these are not a common or widespread habitat. It is probably fair to say that in general the larger more open woods and forests are preferred to smaller tracts, but, as well as density, the height and age structure of the trees and the consequent amount or extent of the undergrowth are important to the bird. In some areas, particularly towards the north and east (i.e. within the ranges of *abietinus* and *tristis*), where the larger tracts of forest give way to areas where willows and alders predominate, wetter habitats are used more frequently than in the central or southern parts of the range. In northern Britain, nominate Chiffchaffs have shown a preference for trees and woods which have been underplanted with (or have become invaded by) rhododendrons, which not only give shelter but are also a good provider of insect food.

In Germany, studies undertaken by Schönfeld (1980) show that for differing habitats there are varying density levels: for example, in parks and cemeteries with mature trees there were as many as 200 pairs per square kilometre, and in riverine woods, notably of alder and elm, populations could often be as high as 128 pairs per square kilometre. In the Bialowieza forest of eastern Poland, studies carried out by students from Warsaw University of the bird communities in differing habitats showed that there are between two and 12 pairs of Chiffchaffs per square kilometre of oak-hornbeam forest, eight pairs per square kilometre of mixed conifer and broadleaf forest, up to ten pairs per square kilometre of pine with bilberry undergrowth, and between 26 and 47 pairs per square kilometre of ash-alder woods and forest which increases to about 54 pairs per square kilometre as the habitat changes to alder swamp forest. These are perhaps slightly exceptional and reflect the highest densities in what are, after all, probably the best examples of prime habitat for the bird. Elsewhere, densities in different habitats are somewhat lower. In south-west Bohemia, in Czechoslovakia, a study of the birdlife in the various woods and forests on peat bog found a range of between 27 and 55 pairs of Chiffchaffs, while deciduous forests in Germany supported a huge range difference from three pairs up to a maximum of 60 pairs per square kilometre which was reflected in France by the range of 2–109 pairs per square kilometre occupying oak copses and shelterbelts and between 4–114 pairs in the same-sized area of coppice woodland.

Densities in forests which are comprised mainly of fir with occasional glades of birch are comparatively low, but appear to depend on the latitude. In a pine forest in north-east France the density recorded was about 30 pairs per square kilometre, while further north the densities in similar habitat in Finland are only between four and 14 pairs for the same-sized area (in some areas even this figure may be considered as high, since previous studies in Finland of the same habitat have found only three pairs per square kilometre). In mixed conifer and broadleaf forests in Finland where it was found that the density was comparable with that of mostly pine forest, at about 12 pairs per square kilometre.

Further east, studies of the habitat requirements of *tristis* showed mixed woods and forests around Pskov, western Russia, to hold an average density of about 5.5 pairs per square kilometre, whereas more open mixed forests with glades and breaks in the cover, such as rides, had a higher density of between nine and 12 pairs. In northern Russia, a study of forests in the Pechora river area found a wide difference in territory occupation in the differing forests, from less than two pairs per square kilometre in the thicker forest which let in insufficient light to allow a good understorey to develop to slightly over 30 pairs per square kilometre in areas of more widely spaced spruce trees with a good ground cover of moss. There is generally very little information on the density of birds within the Siberian forests, but Khaklov (1937, in Dementiev and Gladkov 1951–54) published records which stated that the Chiffchaff was one of the commonest breeding birds of the taiga belt, becoming progressively rare towards the north and east of the range; the only figures quoted were from the region of Salair, where there was one pair per 2–12 hectares.

Birds of the race *brehmii* clearly favour the natural habitats found at higher levels rather than the preferences shown by the more northerly-breeding races. Throughout Spain and Portugal, and to a certain extent in the outposts in North Africa, the birds of this race breed at a higher altitude than elsewhere, in the cork oak forests and the open forests of mixed oaks and chestnut, above which they are also found in mixed scrub and open heath. In some of the high sierras where the terrain is steep and rugged the birds nest in the woodlands of encinas and cork oaks that have a well-developed ground layer of cistus scrub. At lower levels some may breed in the valley woodlands, but this habitat is more widely used in winter, when Chiffchaffs of both this and the nominate race move down to lower levels, including the coastal regions, throughout much of southern Spain. In the temperate woodlands of the meso-Mediterranean type densities are particularly high, with between 14 and 21 birds per 10 ha of holm oaks and *Quercus cerris* in the southern Sierra de Gredos, approximately eight birds per 10 ha in the cork woods of the Sierra Moreno, and about 12 birds per 10 ha in the pines and scrub in Dōnana.

On the western Canary Islands, Chiffchaffs of the race *canariensis* show preferences for the habitats of both the western race *collybita* and the eastern *tristis* in selecting woods with tall trees and a good undergrowth layer, parkland shrubberies or large gardens and also favouring the native (and introduced) pine woods which are generally at higher elevations and well spaced with a good ground layer of (frequently) tangled vegetation. E. A. R. and D. Ennion spent some time on the north coast of Tenerife in January and February 1961 and reported that Chiffchaffs were fairly common and appeared to have a density (at sea level or in most of the low-lying areas) of about one pair to every 4-5 ha. Other studies of *canariensis* on Tenerife, carried out by L. M. Carrascal (1987), show that at higher elevations there is a clear preference for *Pinus radiata*, where the densities recorded were up to 119 birds per square kilometre, compared with 23 birds in the same-sized area of the native *Pinus canariensis*; in plantations of younger pine trees (unspecified) the densities were also higher than in the more mature native trees, averaging of just over 36 birds per km^2.

The only information available on the race *exsul*, which lived in one valley on Lanzarote in the Canary Islands, is that it occurred in much the same type of habitat as that of its close relative and neighbour, *canariensis*, but was also found on the edge of cultivated areas in small trees and shrubs, particularly fig trees.

It was a long-held belief by the early British ornithologists that wherever the two species occurred together the Chiffchaff was less numerous than the Willow Warbler because the latter was slightly larger and (presumably) more aggressive in competing for breeding territory. We now know that this is not the case at all and that the numbers are closely related to the availability of habitat, or even the type of nesting habitat preferred by either species within a larger area of seemingly ideal habitat for both species. Studies carried out by Eric Simms (1985) found that most of the pedunculate oak woods in England held breeding pairs of Chiffchaffs, but in woods which held both species the Willow Warbler invariably outnumbered the Chiffchaff, usually by at least four to one, but in some cases by as much as eight or ten pairs of Willow Warblers to one of Chiffchaffs, again demonstrating the wider level of habitat occupation or tolerance of habitat change or development by Willows over that of Chiffchaffs. Other long-term studies carried out by Beven (1976) at Bookham Common in Surrey showed that, in developing woods which held high numbers of Willow Warblers and comparatively few Chiffchaffs, the ratios changed as the trees matured and the Willows declined in numbers while the numbers of Chiffchaffs remained stable.

As an indication of the Chiffchaff's preference for conifers in the eastern part of the range and the avoidance of this habitat by Willow Warblers, Turcek (1956) found that in the spruce forests of eastern Slovakia Chiffchaffs were the second commonest species, with 43 birds per 100 ha compared with 56 Goldcrests and followed by 20 Wood Warblers and a total absence of Willow Warblers.

On migration the Chiffchaff can be found almost anywhere although once the birds breeding on higher ground and montane areas have departed it is unlikely, certainly in Europe, that many will be found at any

An open woodland with tall trees and a good vegetation cover at ground layer is crucial for breeding Chiffchaffs.

great altitude. In northern Europe, following the breeding season it becomes a nomadic individual roaming at will wherever it is most likely to find food. For the most part this will still involve trees, copses and woods, but many will have deserted the great forests by the end of the summer in search of more open ground. At this time of year it can appear in towns and city gardens or small parks and gather in small or loose flocks, especially where there is an abundance of insect food. At certain coastal sites it occurs in willow saplings, tamarisks, reedbeds and bushes (particularly brambles and elderberry) and feeds wherever insects are found, even in the sparsest vegetation. These flocks often consisting of first-year birds, show little obvious allegiance to each other (although many are in fact related) but clearly have an affinity, since it is not unusual for them to utter contact calls at regular intervals.

As the autumn progresses, these flocks and individuals move south or south-westwards, either in a slow rambling fashion and almost literally from tree to tree or by longer overnight flights. On the coasts of Scandinavia, the Baltic Republics and elsewhere in northern Europe, it is not unusual to see considerable numbers congregating at departure or arrival points. At this time of the year they become nervously active and restless, frequenting any type of habitat from gravel pits to shingle spits, headlands and peninsulas and coastal gardens which may hold a temporary attraction for them or for insect prey which they require in order to lay down a layer of fatty tissue for the longer journey ahead.

Around the Mediterranean, the Chiffchaff occurs on passage in almost any kind of coastal or lowland habitat, from ground-level scrub and bushes to clumps of trees on hills, headlands and along river valleys. In parts of south-west Europe and the Middle East, it occurs in hillside maquis scrub and in orchards and edges of cultivation, particularly where there is good feeding. Further east, it occurs in isolated bushes and clumps of vegetation at the edges of the large deserts and dry country areas of southern central Asia. Birds on passage south or south-east through the mountainous areas of central Asia and which have to cross the high barriers of the Tien Shan and Himalyayan ranges generally move through the lower valleys and follow the courses of streams and rivers, stopping to rest or refuel in any available cover, mostly in small woods or clumps of trees or bushes; at higher levels they follow drier watercourses, and can be seen on occasions in low or rather stunted vegetation on the top of high ground, usually pausing only briefly, possibly for a day or so, before moving on.

In their winter quarters, too, Chiffchaffs occupy a greater variety of habitats than in the breeding season. Some may make a short-distance movement to Mediterranean citrus orchards or date plantations, olive or carob groves, large gardens (usually near woodland) or an area of maquis or garrigue thickets or scrubland, while others show a preference for open country with bushes.

In the more southerly parts of the wintering area, particularly that of nominate *collybita*, the birds take to using palm groves and well-watered areas, especially irrigated areas such as the edges of cultivations, vineyards and hotel gardens. In Spain, considerable numbers winter in both pine forests and cork oak woods as well as lowland woods and copses throughout Andalucia and Extremadura. In Morocco, a great many winter in the cork oak woods of the middle Atlas range and also at lower altitudes in small woods of both conifer and mixed broadleaf; along rivers and wadis coming out of the Sahara the species winters in scrub and fairly thick thornbush vegetation of no great height, and frequently occurs in coastal date palms and the oases of the northern Sahara. In Turkey, up to 300 - 400 winter in the coastal scrub of the south and west, with a few also around some of the larger inland lakes.

In most of the Middle East the Chiffchaff is principally a passage migrant, but it can be found in some numbers in winter at certain locations. Around the Azraq oasis in Jordan, birds of both *collybita* and *abietinus* races are found mostly in the tamarisk and other medium-level shrubs and bushes close to the water's edge. In Israel, individuals of both races spend the winter in the pine forests of the middle-level altitudes and are also found in coastal areas of maquis, bushy scrub and edges of cultivation and gardens. Recent surveys by Meininger *et al.* (1989), carried out in the Egyptian part of the Sahara, also found both races wintering there, although *collybita* was by far the commoner. In this area densities vary from 2-4 birds per kilometre in November to up to ten per kilometre in February, and the surveys concluded that 'on the basis of these figures tens of thousands of Chiffchaffs winter in the Eastern Desert alone'.

For those birds wintering in North Africa, either in the olive groves and date palms on the edge of the desert or in the scattered wadis and oases throughout the vast stretches of the Sahara desert, there will be little choice in the habitat, which becomes secondary to the abundance of food and the presence of life-giving water. In the winter months during 1978-82, P. W. Browne carried out surveys of the Palearctic passerines wintering in seven differing types of habitat in Mauretania and found that most wintered in well-vegetated areas varying from scattered bushes to acacia scrub, but always where there was water present. These areas were mainly small or temporary pools and lakes that appear following the rains and gradually dry up as the dry season advances. In such areas the Chiffchaff shares the habitat with a range of other Palearctic migrants which have moved south for the winter, including White Storks, Glossy Ibis, Garganey, Marsh Sandpipers, Snipe, Temminck's Stints, Sand Martins, Yellow Wagtails, Red-throated and Tree Pipits and Nightingales.

Along the southern edge of the Sahara, Chiffchaffs winter in isolated oases and towards the coast along rivers. In Mali and Niger they also occur in the extensive areas of swamp along the Niger inundation zone. In the more humid regions at the southerly edge of the range they occur in thornscrub, tamarisks and acacia savanna (particularly *Acacia scopioides*), usually those in or near wet or damp areas, and avoid the open and more arid areas of acacia steppe. In the Gambia and other parts of West Africa they readily take to wintering in mangroves, particularly the relatively low-growing *Avicennia*, and the swamps bordering rivers.

In East Africa, Chiffchaffs, mostly of the race *abietinus*, winter along the Nile and are also found at oases and cultivated areas along the edge of the Red Sea all the way south to at least Djibouti, where they are known to winter in the gardens of the Djibouti Sheraton hotel. Inland, in southern Sudan, Ethiopia and Somalia, they are found at higher elevations than in West Africa, with most records coming from over 1800 m although there are a considerable number of records, possibly of birds lingering on passage, in the Rift Valley of southern Ethiopia. In Kenya and northern Tanzania, most are seen in mountain forests (including those on the slopes of Mt Kilimanjaro) and in bamboo, mainly between 1800 and 3300 m, with occasional records between December to April at up to 3700 m, where they occur in the *Erica arborea* zone. There is a scattering of mid-winter records of birds in isolated areas of northern Kenya, mostly forests and edges of cultivation or bushland below 1400 m, and these become more frequent and widespread (although the species is only locally common or infrequent) across central and western Kenya and eastern Uganda.

The wintering grounds of most Willow Warblers lie much further south in Africa than those of the Chiffchaff. Very few Chiffchaffs cross the equator (certainly none of the nominate race), while most Willow Warblers certainly do. There are, however, some areas in West Africa and down the Rift Valley of southern Ethiopia and north-central Kenya where the two species occur together during the northern winter. The habitat preferences of each species at this time of year are not especially clear but, in the main, Willow Warblers occur in more open habitat in trees, bushes and grassland savannas but are also found in riverine forests; they also occur in mixed-species feeding flocks which rove seemingly at random through lower-altitude forests than those occupied by wintering Chiffchaffs. The Willow Warbler is a bird of much drier habitat than the Chiffchaff and is frequently found in acacia steppe and dry *Brachystegia* woodland, more so than any other Palearctic warbler. In Sierra Leone, it occurs in the extensive grassy savannas and swamps where it accompanies another fugitive from the northern winter – the Sedge Warbler.

In Saudi Arabia, Chiffchaffs, mostly of the race *abietinus*, but with eastward progression also *tristis*, winter in oases, date and palm groves and anywhere else which is suitable and provides a feeding area. In northern Oman, F. J. Walker recorded wintering Chiffchaffs in a variety of coastal and lowland scrub habitats but also found them in mangroves; one of the sites in Oman included a sewage farm, where the birds were particularly numerous in the reeds and low vegetation. In North Yemen, birds of the race *tristis* appear to winter in small numbers in the highlands, where they occur in scrub vegetation and small copses and gardens of the main towns and cities, including the capital Sana'a and other areas over 1500 m.

In southern Iran and Baluchistan, Chiffchaffs winter in tamarisk and other hedgerow shrubs. The race *tristis* winters from northern Pakistan to western Bangladesh, generally below 2100 m, and is found, according to Whistler (1928), 'wherever trees are in leaf or cultivation exists'. It occurs both singly and in small or loose parties, often with other species, which search for insects up in the trees, in hedges or in various crops; it appears to be particularly fond of cotton fields, lucerne, tamarisk and acacias, and is also found in scrub jungle or at the edges of large stands of tall trees. It also has a characteristic habit, seldom shared by others of the genus – certainly not so noticeably – of hunting in reedbeds and other vegetation low over water. In the lowlands of Nepal it is a bird of the streamside vegetation, mostly willows and light forest of the edges of the hills.

6

FOOD AND FORAGING

Chiffchaffs, along with virtually every other species of Palearctic warbler, especially those of the small leaf-gleaning *Phylloscopus* genus, are insect-eaters. But it is not so simple as that. The Chiffchaff is not quite as catholic in its choice of food as one might be led to believe.

The Chiffchaff, and most of the other *Phylloscopus* warblers, have a varied diet. The daily food intake, comprising for the greater part of the year insects of one kind or another, is made up of a wide range of (probably in excess of two hundred) species taken from a diversity of micro-habitats. This amply demonstrates that they are not dependent on the success of another single organism but exploit an extensive range of species from a diversity of sources.

Chiffchaffs often feed by hovering on the outer edges of a tree and collect insects from the leaves.

Over 50 families of insects (mainly flies) have been identified as being eaten by Chiffchaffs. These are mainly stoneflies, damselflies, grasshoppers, earwigs, bugs, lacewings, moths, dipteran flies, beetles, aphids, spiders, ants, mites and small molluscs. Studies of the diet of adult birds in Russia have shown that invertebrates in the following orders comprise a considerable part of the daily intake: Hemiptera, Lepidoptera, Diptera, Hymenoptera, Coleoptera and Arachnida. Similar studies have demonstrated that the nestlings are fed on insects and larvae of these orders and also of Ephemeroptera, Odonata, Plecoptera, Hemiptera, Neuroptera, Trichoptera and molluscs. In short, it is fairly safe to say that Chiffchaffs feed on a variety of small to middle-sized flies which are probably indistinguishable in the field (or, for that matter, in the hand) to anyone who is not an entomologist. The list above conceals the fact that they often take biting (as well as non-biting) midges. The eggs and caterpillars of many moths and butterflies are also taken, particularly those of the winter moth *Tortrix viridana*, which periodically occurs in abundance both in the British Isles and on the Continent. At one study site in Moldavia, the parents of one brood of nestlings regularly brought between four and six larvae to the nest at each visit.

Studies of spring migrants in Denmark from mid-April onwards showed the changing composition and numbers of insects taken from year to year by the birds. In mid- to late April 1973, of 119 items found in the stomachs, 66 per cent (by number) were species of Chironomidae, 10 per cent adult Psyllidae and 9 per cent Lepidoptera. A year later, in early to mid-April 1974, the composition had changed slightly: of 166 items, 71 per cent were adult Psyllidae, 9 per cent Chironomidae and 8 per cent Lepidoptera larvae. Of 307 items early May 1973, 52 per cent were Chironomidae and 10 per cent Psyllidae, and by the same time a year later the composition was much the same, with 841 items being found to contain 51 per cent Chironomidae, 28 per cent Psyllidae and 9 per cent Lepidoptera larvae (Laursen 1978).

The Chiffchaff's diet is occasionally supplemented by some plant material. This consists mainly of seeds, berries and occasionally some fruit of *Pistacea*, *Phillyrea*, *Olea*, persimmon *Diospyros*, *Lycium*, bilberrry *Vaccinium*, elder *Sambucus* (including red elder), currant *Ribes*, plum *Prunus* and birch *Betula* (all from Cramp 1992) while Perez-Chiscano (1983) recorded birds eating blackberries (*Rubus*) in Spain. One instance of Chiffchaffs eating fruit is perhaps more worthy of our attention than others. In the autumn of 1979, Bernard Gooch noticed that a small persimmon tree in his garden in northern Portugal had produced its first crop of large orange fruits at the same time as a fairly heavy passage of Chiffchaffs occurred. The birds congregated at the tree and for several weeks 'gorged themselves on the pulp and skin of the ripe persimmons, eating from early morning until evening, with only occasional gaps (not exceeding ten seconds) when none was in the tree; this continued until no fruit remained. A total of at least 20 persimmons, each weighing 110-140 g, was eaten by the warblers. The following year fewer Chiffchaffs were present, and although some persimmons were eaten the birds spent more time feeding in the usual manner. As Barbara and David Snow have commented in their book *Birds and Berries* (1988), one can only speculate about the scarcity of other food or the abnormal concentration of migrants that caused this seemingly unusual outbreak of feeding behaviour.

Chiffchaffs have also been seen taking the nectar of certain plants on the Canary Islands, including poinsettia *Euphorbia*, *Lapeyrousia*, *Eucalyptus* and aloe *Aloe* (Cramp 1992). More significantly, however, birds have been recorded on migration with dried or solidified pollen attached to their bill and forehead or even on the crown.

Among the more unusual food items taken by Chiffchaffs, William C. Tait in *The Birds of Portugal* (1924) records them sipping the nectar of blue gum trees while hovering like hummingbirds. In Khartoum in the Sudan, Pettet (1975) watched a similar instance when an individual repeatedly fed on the crystallized gum exuding from an Acacia tree in November 1964. More recently, wintering Chiffchaffs in Devon have been recorded feeding on dripping-fat and suet-fat put out for birds. A wintering bird in Aberdeen in February was seen by Gavin Forrest on two occasions to pick at peanuts in a wire feeder, on the second occasion it pecked at the nuts before dropping to the ground below the feeder, where it picked up and ate several fragments of peanuts or scattered birdseed.

Without doubt the Chiffchaff is an opportunistic feeder, a bird that feeds on whatever species of insect it can get whenever it is available. Most insects once they have reached the adult stage live very short lives (some less than 24 hours), and any insectivorous bird needs therefore to be equipped with a range of options. In high summer there is a great abundance of insect food and the living must, indeed, be easy, but what of the other times of the year? The Chiffchaff's habitat provides a multitude of insects throughout most of the northern summer, which, in mild or good years, can begin as early as March and continue to the end of October – coinciding with the time when the majority of Chiffchaffs are present in the breeding range. Conversely, a late spell of cold or wet weather in April can be fatal to many of the early migrants or even those on newly established territories, and, with the absence of warm weather to stimulate insect life, they are forced to turn to whatever they can get, wherever they may find it. One particularly good example of opportunistic feeding was witnessed by Jeffery Harrison in Kent in early April 1958, when after a heavy fall of snow, he watched a Chiffchaff and a Whitethroat take insects from the surface of a water tank. They constantly flew out from the bank and momentarily held their wings motionless over their backs as they glided along and picked off insects from the surface of the water. After catching an insect they would return to the bank to eat it. Harrison comments that he did not know which bird had discovered this unusual feeding method first, but it continued for well over an hour.

The size, agility and adaptability of the bird allow it to take in a range of insects from a wide selection of micro-habitats. Most external woodland insects or their larvae are found either in leaves or in buds; a whole range more is found in and under the bark or even as wood-borers into the tree itself, but in general these are outside the reach of the bird in question. The

A Chiffchaff feeding by flycatching. This happens frequently on warm, calm days and sunny autumn mornings.

bird's non-stop searching reflects the need constantly to maintain or at certain times in the year even increase its body weight; in early autumn this feeding becomes a frantic exercise to put on more body fat to fuel the long journey to the wintering area or, in the case of more sedentary individuals, to guard it against the period of severe weather and the possibility of a shortage of food.

There have been no studies carried out in Europe which have been able to determine the average daily intake needed to maintain a healthy existence. Studies in Denmark and elsewhere have, however, shown, from the contents of the stomachs examined, what insect species Chiffchaffs were taking and the relative numbers available; unfortunately, what they cannot show (for obvious reasons) is the length of time taken by the bird to collect all the food items. It is perhaps safe to assume that a bird as small as the Chiffchaff, which weighs on average only 7.0–8.5 g (depending on age, sex and the time of year), needs to eat about a third of its own weight every day, e.g. about 2.35 g of insects. Since most insects are so light that they cannot be weighed, this demonstrates the need to consume great quantities, hence the huge amount of time spent daily in the quest.

The problems, or potential problems, of finding enough food are compounded at the onset of the breeding season and by the task of feeding three or four (possibly up to six) young. As discussed later in Chapter 9, one of the chief requirements that the parent birds must consider, and to some extent be able to foresee, is that the territory will be able to support the feeding demands of the growing young. Some research suggests that, for most bird species (certainly for the larger birds of prey), the abundance of prey items determines the fitness and breeding condition of the adult female and possibly also the number of eggs she is able to produce and the consequent number of young the area can viably support. Studies of the food items given to nestlings reveal that most items certainly in the first five-day period are, perhaps not surprisingly, of softer foods, with fewer beetles and more larvae of aphids, together with some small damselflies. The studies in the former USSR found that various species of Lepidoptera, mostly small moths, were given, together with small flies and gnats, spiders, stoneflies and lacewings. The diet varies as the season progresses and with regional differences in prey abundance. In Germany, aphids made up at least 50 per cent of the food items given to second broods.

The normal or average weight of a male Chiffchaff is 7-8 g, while that of a female is slightly lighter, about 6-7 g. This would be the weight in early summer or mid-summer, when the birds need to keep themselves up to an average body weight while finding food for themselves and also feeding the offspring for the next generation, and before they themselves need to consider increasing their food intake in preparation for autumn departure or winter hardships. Once the young have become fully fledged the adults undergo a complete moult of feathers, and at this stage they look very drab and dowdy as the old feathers, most of which have been worn since the middle of the previous winter, are gradually replaced. At this time they become very quiet and spend long periods, mostly in the middle of the day and early afternoon, asleep or generally inactive. The second half of July is the quietest period of the year for anyone who regularly watches a woodland or patch of common, since most birds, with the exception of one or two early-breeding species, are undergoing a moult of the wing and/or body feathers and have no wish to advertise their presence to any potential predators. Feeding is limited to early mornings and evenings, with only short forays in between. At this time of year, the weight drops by as much as a gram and most Chiffchaffs will be at their lightest, at about 6 or 6.5 g.

Following the moult period by a matter of days or weeks, beginning in late July or early August (depending on the location), comes the period of greatest feeding activity. Foraging and feeding are pursued with renewed vigour, and as daylight hours begin to diminish become virtually the sole activity, with birds feeding from dawn almost through the day until dusk. The result of such a frenzy of feeding is that the weight of some individuals can rise dramatically in a matter of days or weeks. While some will put on only a gram or two to achieve the desired weight of about 7.5-9 g, others, living in areas of high insect activity or infestation, can become visibly much larger, the Billy Bunter equivalent of the Chiffchaff world. Some of these heavyweights may, at the outset of their migration weigh between 9.5 and 10.5 g and extreme weights of 11.2 and 11.5 g are not unknown.

Being heavy does not ensure survival of migration or a long flight during the journey, since weight is not an isolated factor. The overall body weight should not be heavier than is necessary to sustain the bird and to provide for a long flight without the chance of refuelling en route. Once the bird has arrived in its wintering area it will, in most cases, have used most, if not all, of the fat stored for the journey and will be near or just above average weight. Most Chiffchaffs winter in areas with a relatively warm climate, and will need to forage and feed at the normal rate or just below. From the weights of some birds in winter in Cyprus and Algeria, it seems that a lower-than-average weight of about 6-7 g, presumably as a result of warmer temperatures and less consequent loss of body heat, is sufficient to maintain the individual throughout the period.

We have already mentioned an unusual record of a wintering bird in eastern Scotland eating or attempting to eat peanuts. This may have been opportunism (having seen other birds feeding on the peanuts) or it may have been a desperate attempt to obtain sustenance. Other wintering Chiffchaffs in northern Europe must improvise from a reduced range of choices or perish, since it is unlikely that the weather will be mild enough all winter to allow much insect activity. However, if the birds could not survive the northern winter they would not remain there so regularly and in what must amount to considerable numbers.

Foraging methods

Chiffchaffs have short bills which taper to a fine point, which is perfectly designed for foraging for insects or larvae in bark and is finely pointed for picking insects off leaves and for lightly probing into the buds of opening leaves. Its gape is not large, but is large enough to take wasps.

The normal methods of foraging are persistent searching through the canopy or leaf cover of trees or bushes, mainly during migration, and foraging in bushes, low scrub and thickets. Chiffchaffs may compete with Willow Warblers for feeding areas, but they tend to forage higher in the canopy and, although there is an overlap, there appears to be no conflict between the two.

Chiffchaffs move easily through the leafy canopy of deciduous trees and the thicker cover of conifers; such a light bird can easily perch on flimsy twigs and stems to pick off small insects, or search the bark of trees in treecreeper fashion. Another method more commonly or frequently employed by some of the smaller *Phylloscopus* warblers, such as. Pallas's, is hovering a few millimetres from leaves or blossoms too deep or distant to reach by perching, usually on the outside of trees, and picking the food items from leaves, buds etc. At other times on warm days or in sheltered areas (particularly in winter), the birds flycatch from bushes and small trees by darting or dashing after small (often invisible to the human eye) flies which are circling in the warm air a metre or two from the bush.

Birds on breeding territory feed within a defined area. Migrants on passage also often feed in a regular circuit, searching bushes and trees systematically before moving on to the next in line and then making a return visit to the same trees or bushes. Apart from the regularity of food likely to be found within a certain area, it is not certain why this method is adopted: many birds appear to search the same areas in subsequent visits, but presumably a constant supply of food is likely. However, on days when the air is cold or the wind is strong, larger areas or circuits are covered than on days when feeding conditions are good.

On migration and probably at other times in the year, Chiffchaffs feed low down in vegetation or on the ground. Migrants on treeless headlands or islands have to feed in whatever vegetation is present, and it is not unusual to see them feeding low down in scrub or other low-lying vegetation. The wintering habitat over much of the range seems to be much lower than that used in the breeding season; in the Sahel zone of the southern Sahara, Chiffchaffs winter in short riverine scrub and stunted willows.

7

VOICE

Undoubtedly one of the best-known aspects of the Chiffchaff is its song. The Chiffchaff is one of the heralds of spring. In the still and quiet woods, copses and forests of northern Europe at the end of winter, the first stirrings of spring are often accompanied by the first male Chiffchaffs pushing northwards with the retreat of winter and giving short bursts of song from the still leafless trees and saplings coming into bud. The period of song reaches a peak during the spring and early summer, through the display and nesting period and declines in intensity and duration in middle to late summer when the female is rearing the brood. At other times of the year the bird is either less vocal or, on calm autumn mornings, can be induced by the warming rays of early morning sun to give a few, brief, almost half-hearted refrains while taking a short break from foraging or spending a few days off passage. Later in the autumn its thin and somewhat mournful 'sweet' or 'hweet' call note reflects the passing of the northern summer and the departure of most birds from their breeding grounds and is heard less and less until the first returning birds arrive back in early spring.

Song

To the attentive listener, the song is neither simple nor merely a straight repetition of the name. There is rhythm to it, with a momentum created by the seemingly alternating notes complementing each other in quick succession, so that the actual 'chiff-chaff' is lost or obscured within the overall phrases which are run together in a 'chiff-chaff-chiff-chiff-chaff-chiff-chiff-chiff'. The momentum is created by the upward inflection on the 'chiff' and a downward response of the 'chaff' which are often run together as a delightful or pleasant song. Neither is it always a simple matter of repeating its name. The bird often begins its song with a brief, soft (and usually audible only at close range) but also fairly sharp or harsh 'trr'or 'err', or a slightly longer 'churr', but in some cases has been noted as a 'tret' or 'kre'. This note, often repeated, lasts only a second or so before the bird begins its 'chiff-chaff' phrases. This dry preface or introduction to its song is normally recorded only when the bird is on breeding territory but has been recorded on rare instances when on migration, and Chiffchaffs still on passage in late spring have been known to utter it, presumably stimulated by the time of year or by other birds which are on territory.

As with most bird species, the male is the songster of the pair, with the female more limited in her vocabulary. There are, however, a few isolated records or instances which suggest that some females do on rare occasions

give a faint rendering of the song. At the beginning of the male's song period, which in Britain lasts from about the middle of March to September, the song is often delivered hesitatingly or in a rather halting fashion. Later in the spring, the more usual song will be the normal, and usually faster, 'chiff-chaff' or 'tsiff-tsaff', but the jumbled version of the same notes can also be heard and there seem to be no firm rules observed by the bird as to which is given. In some cases, the song is given with such emphasis that it rises towards the middle of the phrase and the notes become shorter or truncated, as 'chiff-chaff-chiff-chaff-chit-it-sooit-sooit'. In German the Chiffchaff is more onomatopoeically referred to as 'zilp-zalp', which, again, is an almost exact rendering to human ears of the song.

There are a number of records of oddly singing Chiffchaffs. The Witherby *Handbook* (1938–41) states that there is an uncommon variant of the Chiffchaff song which closely resembles all or part of a Willow Warbler's song and is preceded or followed by the normal song. Such instances have on occasion led to widespread reports of hybridization with Willow Warblers, but the singers have, on further examination, been proved to be Willows (this is not to say that the two species do not hybridize in rare instances: see Chapter 10). A number of documented records of Chiffchaffs with unusual songs do, however, exist. Walpole-Bond (1938) records one bird giving a 'cheeve-cheeve' note in place of the usual double-note call. In more recent years, other authors have described similarly peculiar songs. R. S. R. Fitter heard a bird singing in Middlesex in June 1942 in which the normal 'chiff-chaff' notes were interspersed with strange 'chee-ouee' notes and a trill recalling a Chaffinch, Redstart or Lesser Whitethroat, the song being rendered as 'chee-ouee, chee-ouee, chee-ouee, chiff-chaff, chiff-chaff, wee-wee-wee-wee, chee-ouee, chee-ouee'. Another record concerns a Chiffchaff in Dorset in April 1959 which seemed to have forgotten the second part of its normal song when singing to proclaim its territory and gave a version rendered as 'chi-chi-chi-chi-chi-churru-churru-chi-chi-chi-chi-chi'; the observers noted that the phrases were quite unlike the normal song, being more decisive, and the middle section was slower, lower-pitched and more thrush-like in its richness.

On the other side of the equation is the recorded evidence by R. A. Frost of a Willow Warbler, identified in the field by shape and coloration, which held a territory in South Yorkshire from 1980 to 1982 and sang seemingly faultless songs of both Willow Warbler and Chiffchaff. A similar instance was documented by S. Haftorn of a Willow Warbler occasionally giving the song of a pure Chiffchaff in Trondheim, central Norway, in July 1983. Haftorn gave similar records of a 'mixed' singer in Scandinavia and also one in Germany. In such instances the song began with that of the alien species and concluded with that proper to the species; however, it is entirely possible, as was in fact demonstrated by the bird in Trondheim, that the Chiffchaff involved can reverse the order and start with its correct song, followed by that of the alien species. Just to confuse the issue, a bird with Chiffchaff-type phrases included within and following a normal Willow Warbler song was recorded in a study area near Lothian in April 1984. This bird had been colour-ringed as a nestling in 1982 and reared by a male Chiffchaff and a female Willow Warbler. Proof of mixed parentage was lacking, but it seems likely that this bird was a true hybrid.

Structure and duration of songs

When used to proclaim territory or advertise for a mate the song can be given for about 15 seconds or slightly longer, but very few Chiffchaffs actually sing for much longer without breaking off or pausing, presumably to draw breath. The length of each song, and the pauses between them, are entirely dependent on the season, the message being sent and the state of excitement shown by the bird. Unmated birds on territory are usually most vocal and sing for an average of less than 15 seconds, and some for a considerably shorter period of only up to 5 seconds, followed by intervals of up to 10 seconds before resuming, but the period of the day devoted to singing (or advertising presence on territory) is much longer than for paired males. From information gathered from a survey of just over 19,000 song phrases given by eight different Chiffchaffs in Britain undertaken in the summers of 1948 and 1949, slightly fewer than half that number were found to be of less than five seconds; at the other end of the range, the same survey found instances of birds singing for up to half a minute. In a separate instance, an individual was recorded in southern England which sang for a record-breaking 48 seconds.

Across Europe and in parts of the former USSR, a number of studies have looked at the structure and variation of the songs of individual Chiffchaffs and studied the recordings of songs either through slowed-down playback or by using sonagrams. Such studies have revealed subtle changes in tone and variations that the human ear is unable to pick up or identify; to many, the song is a somewhat monotonous or metronome-like 'chiff-chaff' repeated or given in a discord of 'chiff-chaff-chaff'-type patterns. What the tapes and graphs reveal, however, is that within the song structure are slight variations of the message being given by the bird and that within the notes which are rendered as (or to our ears sound like) 'zelp' are more slurred notes such as 'zlp'. One individual singing male was found to give 47 different songs with varying sequences of notes. To human ears this may well be inaudible, but to another Chiffchaff it could mean the difference between attraction and aggression.

Songs of the different races

In northern Europe and across to the Urals, the songs of nominate *collybita* and *abietinus* are virtually identical. In northern Turkey, birds of the uncertain race *brevirostris* have a similar song to that of its two northern relatives but slightly harsher and with a more abrupt or clipped 'chiff-chaff' and in parts of the range their song is said by some observers to be distinctly faster than that of either *collybita* or *abietinus*.

The repeated and clear-cut 'chiff-chaff' is certainly absent from the song of males of the race *brehmii*, which has an entirely different song structure. By far the most characteristic or noticeable difference in the song of this race is its halting or slower delivery. Simms, in his monograph *British Warblers* (1985), gave a good representation of the song as a slow but accelerating 'tit-tit-tit-tit-tit-tswee-tswee-chit-it-it-it-it'. The introductory notes also differ from those of both the nominate race and *abietinus*, tending more towards a dry 'chep' or 'jep'; these notes often form part of the song and are given with some emphasis. The song also includes several 'sweet'-type notes (variably given as 'sooid' or 'swiid' to 'treep'), which are a repetition of the high-pitched call notes.

The difference in structure also extends to a variation (perhaps even a dialect in some areas) of the lengths of the phrases contained within the song, so that some birds may extend the trilling notes or the higher-pitched 'sweet' notes or omit them altogether. Despite some evidence of regional dialectic variation of the songs of this race, there appears to be no widespread variation in the structure, so that the songs of *brehmii* in southern Spain are the same as those from south-west France. At the northern end of the range of *brehmii* (usually defined as the French side of the Pyrenees), there is an overlap zone where *brehmii* interbreeds with birds of the nominate race; the song of these hybrid individuals seems to be a confused or mixed jumble of notes with a general resemblance to that of *brehmii*, but there is a considerable degree of variation within the birds in this area. Chiffchaffs in the southern outposts of the breeding range of this race, in the hills and mountains of North Africa have some slight differences, with slower, more halting songs and with a slower rate of declension towards the end.

There have been a small number of records of birds of the Spanish race *brehmii* occurring well to the north of their usual range. Most, if not all, of these occurrences have been of spring birds overshooting their breeding area and these have been identified by song, which, in a bird that is so variable even within its races, is the most distinctive feature. There have been two records of this race in England, in Middlesex in June 1972 and in Dorset in April 1983; a third bird which uttered some Tree Pipit-like notes (as well as the usual 'chiff-chaff' phrases) was considered to be a mixed singer and probably from the overlap zone between the two races. There have also been occurrences of single singing individuals in France (near Paris), Belgium and the Netherlands.

The song of *canariensis* consists of a complex structure and with deeper timbre or pitch than that of *collybita*. Some observers have likened the richness or depth of the song to that of a Chaffinch, while others have considered the song as an almost monosyllabic series of 'chip' notes or a 'chip-cheep-cheep-chip-chip-cheep' with little variation between the two notes and some notes recalling the sharpness of a sparrow's 'chirp'; in some cases, possibly as an indication of a paired bird, the song can be varied slightly to 'chlip-chlip-chuip-chuip'. Some individuals may occasionally begin the song with an explosive note recalling a Cetti's Warbler, such is the intensity of the singer. Knecht, who made a series of recordings of this race in the late 1950s, described the song as 'dschi-dsche-sche-schi-sche-schi-schi' and accelerating towards a brief or somewhat unexpected conclusion. Other singers may decelerate during the course of the song, but most observers are agreed that the overall pitch is lower than that of its northern relatives, but the speed of delivery is generally faster.

As with nominate *collybita* and *abietinus*, the territorial song of Chiffchaffs in this race, which is entirely sedentary and can sing as early as January, is frequently preceded by a short and subdued introductory note. In the main, this has been recorded as 'tuk' or 'chek' but can also be a soft 'che', usually given once before the start of the song but also repeated to form a phrase of its own. The length of the song varies but is usually much shorter than those of the northern birds and lasts on average for approximately 10–12 seconds, with individual phrases of between two and four seconds repeated and with gaps or pauses between bursts of song. As indicated above, with birds giving a song that either accelerates or decelerates during its delivery, there is a considerable amount of variation, even among individuals occupying a small area.

The song of Chiffchaffs of the race *tristis* is considerably different in its tonal quality and is more of an attractive and melodious and flowing warble, but rather high-pitched and somewhat squeaky. It is generally less broken into clear phrases and has a more varied musical repertoire than that of *collybita*. It has recently been transcribed, accurately in my opinion, by the Swedish recorder Ullman as an elegant song, with a marked emphasis roughly on every third syllable: 'suITsitsuITsiuwitssITsiuwITsi'.

The full song is a complex structure beginning with up to three short phrases or subphrases and followed by a series of rather fast, rising and falling tonal notes in twos and threes. According to H. G. Alexander, writing in the early 1950s, the song of *tristis* is best expressed as 'wi-di, wee-di, wee-di, wee, widi, wee', and variations on this are described in Glutz von Blotzheim and Bauer's *Handbuch der Vogel Mitteleuropas* as 'tschiwi tschiwi tschiiwi', or 'tschiwet tschiwit' and 'ip-tschip ip-tschiip tschip-tschiiep tschip tschiiep'. The initial or introductory notes are often a soft 'chiv-it' or 'soo-ip' before following on with the rest of the song. Examination of slowed-down recordings or sonagrams shows that the pattern of short, quickly rising notes followed by a longer falling note is very much the same as that shown by both nominate and *abietinus* birds, although the human ear is oblivious to this.

The introductory notes to the territorial or display song of *tristis* are also recognizable in comparison with those uttered by its western relatives.

The short or dry, husky opening 'tek', 'tret' or 'trr' notes of *collybita* and *abietinus* are replaced in *tristis* by a variable 'tet' or 'tert' note, or, according to the German researcher Mauersberger, by a harsher repeated 'dzrrr-dzrrr-dzrrr', or, as noted by the Polish researchers Aniola and Gorski, a more stuttering 'dr-t dr-t'. This is followed by a slightly faster and more rhythmic 'bu-tk-tk', which can be repeated up to eight times and serves as a preamble to the main rising and falling series of phrases which make up the main song. The song is as varied in tone and structure as are those of the other races but, although seemingly more complex, it contains a smaller number of variable notes (an average of just over 20 notes per song) than in either the nominate or *abietinus* races.

Songs of Chiffchaffs described as belonging to the disputed race *'fulvescens'*, mostly from the western part of the range of *tristis*, differ little (if at all) from typical *tristis* and probably fall within the range of variation shown by the latter race. In northern Russia, Leonovich carried out research on birds holding territory on the Kanin peninsula and found *abietinus* and *tristis* birds singing from separate, adjoining territories and, perhaps more importantly, one male alternately singing the songs of both.

There are a number of European records of *tristis* (see chapter 10) some involving singing individuals. In March 1974, one was heard singing near Hilversum in the Netherlands, and in January 1980, another song near Cheltenham, Gloucestershire. More recently, C. D. R. Heard (1989) has reported song 'occasionally, on sunny late autumn days (in Scilly) and once from a spring migrant (in south Bucks)'. He also records that the song given is distinctive, with the more varied and rambling structure sometimes recalling the 'cadence' of a Willow Warbler and transcribed (by him) as 'weechoo weechoo chewee choo' and 'chivy-chooee chivy-chooee djiff'.

Territory, courtship and display songs

At the height of the display period (typically April to the middle of May for *collybita*, possibly slightly later or more prolonged for birds breeding at the northern edge of the range, particularly *tristis*), the songs of some individuals can be given with a faster rate of delivery or a noticeable emphasis placed on certain passages. Most of this is due to the state of sexual excitement of the male, brought about either by pursuit of a female or by aggressive rivalry shown by song-chases or pursuit of an intruding or nearby male (which may be singing or silent). In certain areas of the range where the density of breeding pairs is quite high, males will often indulge in concert-singing, not for the benefit of the listener but more as a response to a competitive-like stimulus. Males in pursuit of females as part of the courtship utter excited but short or terse 'tret' or 'chit' notes. During the brief but frequently repeated display flight of the male, these notes become more slurred, or even a thin 'chiff-iff-iff' is given, and in some cases of high-intensity display this becomes a chirping 'zierzier-zier'. In the ensuing chase of the female by the male, a series of these short and intense calls is given

Wing-barred Chiffchaff and similar confusion species.

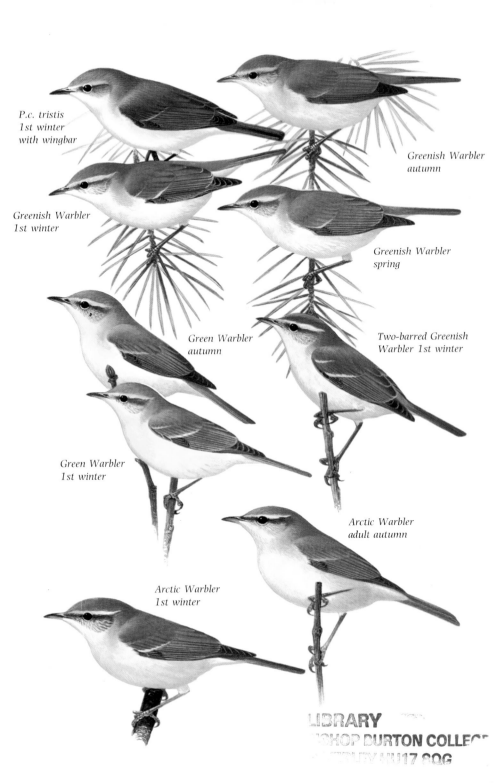

P.c. tristis
1st winter
with wingbar

Greenish Warbler
autumn

Greenish Warbler
1st winter

Greenish Warbler
spring

Green Warbler
autumn

Two-barred Greenish
Warbler 1st winter

Green Warbler
1st winter

Arctic Warbler
adult autumn

Arctic Warbler
1st winter

as part of the increasing attraction and intimacy between the two prior to the bonding of the pair; these calls can also include variations given and include short bursts of 'ziff-ziff' or 'ziet-zief' or a lightly piping 'tu-tu-tu'.

Both sexes respond to each other during the courtship stage with a variety of short contact notes such as a 'drit', 'dit' or 'djick' sound. Other similar contact notes have been recorded from breeding birds. At a long-term study site on Bookham Common in Surrey, Beven found that females often gave a soft 'soliciting' or advertising 'siff-siff', which is very similar to calls described as 'zig zig zag' and 'trip trip het' used by the female and male respectively as contact notes between the two. Beven also records that the female's 'soliciting' or advertising call can produce a responsive high-pitched 'si-si si' from the male as part of the pre-coital display and that this can be repeated several times in succession (but not always resulting in copulation) followed by a period of full song by the male. Other quiet notes seemingly used solely by the female include a series of 'trit' or 'tick' notes when engaged in a distraction or lure display and a quiet 'ett' uttered either during the construction of the nest and also when feeding young (both sexes give quite hard 'tik' or muttered 'tk' notes when feeding the young). Williamson noted a harsh 'chi chi chep' from one female attacking a male which was presumably an interloper and not her mate.

Normal courtship or display song of a male on territory is an excited or extended period of singing often beginning as a low and thin, but sibilant 'tsiff-tsiff-tsiff' when a female is close by before becoming the fuller 'chiff-chaff' song; should the female move to a different bush or tree the male will follow, still singing and imposing his presence on her. Variations on this song have been noted as slightly higher pitched or more metallic in tone, in some cases described as a slightly descending 'tzink tzink tzink'.

Most song, especially that given for courtship or territory-advertising, is delivered from the top of a fairly tall tree which is usually situated at or near the middle of the proposed territory. Most birds sing some way down from the highest point. Treetop singing is not at all unusual, and this may be just one of the vantage points used by the bird as part of a number of singing spots spread throughout the territory which he visits periodically on a set route. Early-morning songsters are perhaps more likely to favour the tops of trees, primarily to catch the first warming rays of the sun and to advertise to any newly arrived females within the area that a prospective mate is present. The male sings either purposefully sitting on an exposed twig at or near the top of the tree, surveying his immediate territory and singing for fairly brief periods interrupted by the urge to feed, or perhaps mainly while foraging and only occasionally breaking off his song to pursue a passing insect or briefly to preen. When singing, the body is almost upright, the head is held at a slightly upward angle and continually turned his head from side to side, the throat feathers are puffed out, and the tail is rhythmically flicked up and down in time with the song. The song can be delivered while the singer is stationary, moving through the treetops, walking along branches or foraging, or even in flight. Near human habitation Chiffchaffs have been known to sing from telephone wires, television aerials and the ridges of roofs.

There seems to be no time of day when the song is not given, but mornings, particularly early mornings on warm, fine days are favoured. As the morning progresses the song period declines slightly (depending on the weather) but increases somewhat to a secondary peak of performance at around midday, thereafter declining rather rapidly in the early afternoon until little or no song at all is heard during the 'mid-afternoon nap' period of most birds in summer, when all but the most lively and vigorous of songbirds are silent. All-day singers are most likely unpaired males. Towards evening song may again be heard, but with somewhat less intent or with longer pauses between bursts than earlier in the day.

In common with most other birds, female Chiffchaffs do not as a rule sing, although there are exceptions to this general rule. A female in Kent in April 1975 was noted by D. Taylor giving two to three phrases of the typical song while nest-building, and Homann records females more regularly uttering short 'chiff-chaff' phrases of song, one noticeably so when she was approaching her nest. It seems that utterances of song by the female Chiffchaff may be stress-related: J. R. King (1992) cited an instance where a couple of phrases of the normal song were given in response to a threat, in one case the absence of the male (temporarily removed by trapping for examination) from the territory and the taped presence of an unknown male inducing the female to sing briefly, and in Taylor's observation, mentioned above, the observer was very close to (apparently within 1 m of) the nest which was under construction.

Following the breeding season the adults go into a period of moult and during this period, in July and early August, the males become quiet and somewhat shy or unobtrusive, preferring not to advertise their presence. Towards the middle or end of August there is a resumption of song by males, albeit in a more half-hearted style than in spring, largely stimulated by warm days, high-pressure-system temperatures and calm or balmy weather inducing birds to linger off passage. It is also noticeable that the song is less frenetic or vigorous than in spring. Some winter songsters have been recorded as delivering vigorous songs, and others have followed this burst of song with a low or soft warble as a subsong. Kenneth Williamson, one of the great pioneers of Palearctic warbler identification and their relationships reported one Chiffchaff in Kenya giving a twittering 'see-see-seeoo-seeoo' quite unlike its summer refrain. In India, wintering *tristis* generally sing from taller trees. In France, south of the Loire, Delamain (1938) noted that Chiffchaffs sing 'softly, as if to themselves'. Elsewhere, there are records from North Africa, the Middle East and around the Mediterranean of Chiffchaffs singing in the period from December to March. In southern England there are now a number of records of wintering birds singing, although the song is simpler, mostly just a repeated 'chiff-chaff', as opposed to the more developed song later in the year.

Calls

Chiffchaffs of the nominate race and western populations of *abietinus* have a fairly well-known soft and rather sad-sounding 'hooeet' call (variously

A male Chiffchaff in song in spring.

written as 'hweeet', 'huit' or 'fweet') with the emphasis on the rising 'eet'. It is very similar to one of the main calls of Willow Warbler, which is also rendered as 'hooeet'.

The 'hooeet' call is certainly distinctive to either Chiffchaff or Willow Warbler; although a number of other species such as Redstart and Pied Flycatcher (possibly also some male Chaffinches) have similar notes, none is given in quite the same soft manner. On migration, particularly early in the year, the call is often the first indication of returning migrants, with newly arrived birds eagerly searching for food and stopping only long enough to give the occasional call before scurrying after another passing insect or moving on to inspect another likely spot. This short and (compared with the slightly longer and more distinctly two syllable 'hoo-eet' of Willow) rather monosyllabic call is probably given as a contact-type call, even though lone birds are frequently vociferous and there is no firm evidence that Chiffchaffs always move in collective groups (but see Chapter 10). Variations on this call include even higher-pitched notes, such as 'sweep' or 'tweep', and the more autumnal notes, such as a rather shrill 'sweeoo' (once considered distinctive of the races *abietinus* and *tristis* but see also below) and the even more plaintive 'weep', 'hweep' or even a distinctly two-syllable 'heweet'.

To the inexperienced listener, the calls of eastern Chiffchaffs of the race *abietinus* and those of *tristis* are initially similar to those of nominate *collybita* and there is undoubtedly a high degree of overlap and similarity in the calls of these races. One of the commonest or most noticeably different calls, certainly among birds occur·in western Europe and the British Isles, is in autumn, when the opportunity for comparison with nominate birds arises. Both eastern *abietinus* and *tristis* utter a rather thin and high-pitched, even shrill or slightly discordant 'peep', 'weep', 'peet', 'pseet' or 'cheet' (some authorities claim that this is more frequently the call of *abietinus*, with the longer 'swee-oo' note given by *tristis*). This piping 'peep' or 'weep' is similar to (or the equivalent of) the 'hooeet' note of nominate birds, but is distinctly more plaintive or mournful and has been likened to the distress call of a young chicken or even to that of a Coal Tit. It is certainly much more hollow, mellow or sad in tone, than that of *collybita*. Other notes typical of the eastern Chiffchaffs, particularly *tristis*, are a slightly descending but plaintive 'swee-oo' or 'psee-uu', again recalling a Coal Tit in tone; other *tristis* calls have been described as 'chiv-it' or similar variations on that theme.

The contact call of *tristis* pairs on the breeding grounds is a fairly sharp or piping 'see', 'swee' or 'psee', either uniform in tone or slightly descending; this note is also given by *abietinus* breeding in the Caucasus, but here it is somewhat sharper and more sibilant, recalling a Dunnock. In the race *brehmii*, the contact, excitement and alarm calls are similar to those of nominate birds, but the contact call descends rather than rises in pitch; also, some of the calls given by adult females and immatures in autumn are similar to the shrill or hollow 'peep' or 'weep' of eastern birds. A Chiffchaff, generally accepted as being of this race, which occurred at the Brent Reservoir in north-west London in June 1972 and referred to above (under song) gave a short but repeated 'tic tic tic' as part of its call, possibly an excitement call similar to the 'tret' or 'tick' notes given by nominate-race birds.

The calls of Canary Islands race *canariensis* are close to some of those uttered by *collybita*, particularly the short and sharp 'chirp', 'wheet', 'hwit', 'huit' or 'tuit' excitement or alarm notes; the 'chirp' note is clearly very similar in tone to some of the notes in the song, given above, particularly so when uttered as a double-note. The only information available on the calls of *exsul* comes from the works of Polatzek, who studied the birds of the Canaries in the early years of this century; he described the call as similar to that of *canariensis*, but slightly longer and somewhat harsher.

Alarm calls of Chiffchaffs seem to be very similar among all races (where they are known). In most cases alarm is expressed as a sharp or loud 'fiet', similar in tone to one of the sharp notes used as a contact at the nest. Once uttered, usually at the approach of a predator, the call is very infectious and is taken up by other Chiffchaffs in the vicinity; it is also recognized, probably more by the intensity or sharpness of its delivery, by other species as a sign of distress. In common with other members of the *Phylloscopus* genus, female Chiffchaffs give a low or soft but sharp hissing note or develop this into a continued hiss if disturbed at the nest, and the same is given by the male when driving off a predator. If alarmed or in flight, particularly when encountering a predator or being attacked by a bird of prey, both sexes utter a high-pitched squeak. It is interesting to observe that ground-based predators elicit an alarm call only in the breeding season; at other times of the year the bird remains silent and quietly avoids the presence of the intruder. In eastern *abietinus* and *tristis* birds the same shrill or high-pitched 'pseet', 'peep' or 'weep' call note is given repeatedly as an alarm, particularly at the presence of a predator; other calls from birds of the eastern regions have been noted as a descending variation on the 'swee-oo' call note and a Coal Tit-like 'weeeaa', the latter particularly in autumn and winter.

Nestling and fledgling calls

The calls of nestlings have been studied in depth by Homann (1960) and Gwinner (1961) who found clear differences as the nestlings became older. In the first three days no calls were heard from the chicks. At three days old they gave a sharp 'zi' or 'zie' as a begging call when the parent returned to the nest, which increased in volume and developed into a short series when being fed, or became a slightly harsher or more coarsely delivered 'tschiii-tschiii'. At six days old the begging calls changed to a more drawn-out 'pzrrp' or a variation thereof such as 'pzierp', 'ziep', 'zierp', 'zulp' or 'tschilp' which, as with all young birds in the nest, were given as occasional quiet notes when the chicks were unattended but became louder when the parents were at the nest or were in the vicinity and giving their contact notes. Gwinner's work showed that young Chiffchaffs can easily distinguish the calls of their mother from those of other Chiffchaffs at an early age, and are certainly able to do so by the time they leave the nest. The commonest contact note of the adults is a short 'fut' given mostly by the female or a somewhat louder 'fit' given by both sexes, in some cases extended into a longer 'fiet-at-at-at'; at one nest in southern Germany, the male gave a short 'zieje' before delivering the food to the young and the adults gave a slightly similar 'tiezieh-tiezieh' when both were together at the nest. The need for physical contact or brooding from the adult female is usually expressed by the nestling as a low whispering trill, which can be slightly buzzing in tone, accompanied by a slight shivering of the wings.

Once the young are out of the nest, but still dependent on the parents for food, their calls change slightly or subtly depending on the requirements of the growing bird. When one of the nestlings has become parted from its brothers or sisters (or is unsure where they are), it utters a sharp 'pzierp' which is similar to but subtly different from the higher-pitched 'tschiep' fright call which is given in alarm or distress, for example at having to take flight at an intruder; other alarm calls are a variety of high-pitched or hissing 'che' notes, often repeated or run into a short 'trr'. Other identifiable (but very similar) notes are the short 'trtt', 'tritt' or 'tschrrt' calls related to changes of position (when it could easily be lost in the canopy of a tall tree with an abundance of foliage) and food-begging calls.

Most calls of juvenile or newly fledged Chiffchaffs seem to be rather shrill or sharp or a variation on the high-pitched 'pziep', 'sfie' or even a 'sweeoo' recalling both a young chicken, and, to more experienced ears, the autumn call of Yellow-browed Warbler.

8

BEHAVIOUR

Actions and characteristics

In the Chiffchaff these movements are particularly noticeable in the tail, which is almost continually flicked (a Chiffchaff which does not do this is either tired, unwell or not a Chiffchaff). When foraging and on landing the tail is dipped slightly and then quite purposefully flicked as the bird changes its position; a bird which is stationary will, when deciding on a course of action, flick its tail quickly from time to time. In Chiffchaffs this nervous movement reflects a state of alertness or excitement when feeding, an action not generally shown by Willows, which give only a rather shallow and almost half-hearted dip of the tail when landing or changing perch. In the course of their daily activities both Chiffchaffs and Willow Warblers use a range of perches; in the main these are horizontal or diagonal, but when they are actively feeding they utilize stems and twigs at all angles, even stopping briefly on stones or on the ground.

A foraging Chiffchaff, especially in the early morning, is usually a bundle of nervous energy, ever alert and on the go looking for its next meal and full of vitality and nervous movement with occasional wing-flicks and tail-wags. The Willow Warbler by contrast is somewhat less highly charged or excitable, shows less nervous momentum and generally keeps its tail still while feeding.

Tail-wagging is not only noticeable when the bird is excited or agitated but is also at its most visible or intense when the male is singing. Almost in regular time with the 'chiff-chaff' notes of the song, the tail is wagged up and down and the songster also moves its wings and turns its head from side to side. Wing-flicking in its mildest form is only an occasional part of its behaviour and, although visible from time to time while the bird is foraging, it seems from the evidence available to be a response to a nervous or anxious state such as when a predator or rival is nearby. Both wing-flicking and tail-wagging, or, more appropriately tail-fanning, are part of the threat display or a response principally of the male defending a territory to a perceived threat.

In addition to its seemingly endless amounts of nervous energy most notably shown in its search for food, the Chiffchaff is particularly inquisitive. The Chiffchaff is one of the species of woodland birds that not only responds to the alarm calls of other species but actively goes in search of the intruder or cause of the alarm. The alarm calls of most birds are easy to recognize by their shrill tone and persistency, and the Chiffchaff clearly recognizes those of both Blackcap and Sedge Warbler. There are records of Chiffchaffs joining in scolding parties of other birds to mob an owl found sitting in an exposed position, or when marauding stoats or weasels are clearly intent on making a meal of a ground-nesting bird's eggs or young.

In the early years of this century, when knowledge of our breeding birds and their nests and eggs was gained only by lengthy observation and searching for nests, the Chiffchaff was recognized as one of the birds that was sure to approach and watch every intrusion into its territory and give a plaintive 'hooeet' alarm. Eliot Howard, in his extensive monograph of the British Warblers and their life history, gives several instances of Chiffchaffs being inquisitive as to what was causing a disturbance in the same territory.

Perhaps the most interesting example is in which two Blackcaps newly arrived on breeding territory were engaged in a frantic struggle for domination of the site. They were vigorously flying at and pecking at each other when suddenly a Chiffchaff arrived and also joined in the fray, attacking first one and then the other Blackcap with indiscriminate abandon. During the pauses in the contest, which was accompanied by the clicking of the bills of all three, the Chiffchaff hopped about the combatants watching excitedly for the next bout to begin, and whenever the battle recommenced it would immediately join in. The affray ended only when one of the Blackcaps conceded defeat and submitted.

Some, if not all, male Chiffchaffs, and certainly those in defence of a territory or young, are extremely bold and fearlessly give their own presence away by announcing the presence of a predator, regardless of whether it is an egg thief (such as a Jay), an unwanted interloper (such as a cuckoo) or a hawk. The state of alarm or excitement shown by some individuals can be so intense that they continue to give the alarm call long after the cause of it has departed. In some cases, birds such as Jays, which pose no real threat to the adult birds, will be escorted and 'serenaded' by the Chiffchaff with persistent alarm calls for up to 30 minutes until they have left the territory. For other predators (or predator-like birds) such as cuckoos, cats or rats, different strategies are adopted; stoats as well as rats and cats, are actively and persistently dive-bombed from close quarters, forcing the intruder to duck its head or slink down, although actual contact with such intruders is rare. This real or playful aggression is much more pronounced in Chiffchaffs than in any other member of the warbler family, and is directed not only towards birds which come too close but also towards those that are flying by or that are preening or even sunbathing, including birds as large as thrushes and doves. One of the most extreme instances of this behaviour was recorded by A. P. Radford (1994): in April 1990, in Somerset, he was watching a small bat, probably a pipistrelle, flying in the early afternoon around several oak trees when a Chiffchaff, which had been singing from the trees for several days previously, suddenly gave chase to the bat for about 30 seconds and then broke off, only to return and chase the bat for at least a further 30 seconds before both bat and pursuer disappeared from view.

Cuckoos are actively and aggressively attacked by dive-bombing and pursued vigorously, often with brief contact in flight, until they have left the territory. Sparrowhawks and Kestrels may elicit the same response,

When alarmed by the presence of a predator, Chiffchaffs become aggressive and fearlessly (for their size) mob by dive-bombing any would-be predator.

depending on the amount of warning given by the predators and the proximity to the bird, but the stealth-and-surprise method of a hunting Sparrowhawk often leaves no time for an alert to be raised except in some cases a short high-pitched squeak or hissing note that communicates the alert to others before the threat is passed. Eliot Howard once recorded a Chiffchaff that responded to a Sparrowhawk by giving a slow butterfly-like flight with fairly laboured wingbeats and with legs dangling, and all the time uttering its alarm call. This has been interpreted as a possible distraction-lure by a bird on territory, possibly with dependent young from which the adult was keen to lure the potential predator away.

Reactions to human intruders depend on the time of year and whether there are dependent young or a nest and eggs to defend. During the building of the nest and throughout the incubation period, the sharp alarm call is given at the sight of human intrusion, which, as in the case of other predators, often induces a high state of excitement that can continue for considerable periods of time especially if the intrusion persists. Once it is clear that the humans are entirely oblivious of the birds, the latter may either resume their activites at fairly close range to the human intrusion or move away until the threat has gone. In some cases of deliberate or persistent alarms (from whatever cause), the males become so agitated and anxious that calls are given for a considerable time after the threat has disappeared.

Some Chiffchaffs have responded to human intrusion at or near the nest by 'freezing' where the bird remains stock still for a while to gauge the next move of the intruder and assess whether it has been seen. Some of this freezing depends to a certain extent on a finely balanced decision between the urge to flee and the amount by which it may be camouflaged: fleeing would only bring attention to the bird or its nest. In one case, a female bringing food to the nest froze at the edge of the nest until the intruder moved away. Freezing has also been noted as an immediate response to the sudden appearance at close range of predators such as Sparrowhawks, since to move at such close proximity is more likely to attract the attention of the predator than remaining 'invisible' would.

Reactions of female Chiffchaffs to intruders near the nest have received little attention, largely because females are mainly silent or give little or no visible signs of excitable alarm other than the sharp, plaintive 'hooeet' call. Eliot Howard, however, recorded the reactions of a female at a nest he was keeping under observation: '...her nervousness at any human presence varies very considerably. If you take up a position near the nest at dawn, before she leaves it, she will not be so nervous; if, on the other hand, you are late and arrive while food is being brought, she will sometimes be more nervous, resenting your presence; and again after you have been there some considerable time, she will suddenly be seized with a nervous fit, which takes her sometime to overcome; thus she will work backwards and forwards up to the nest, approaching even to within a few inches, and as rapidly retreating, but unable to apparently summon up the courage to make the final effort to reach it.' Research currently being carried out by M. Rodrigues at Wytham Woods, near Oxford, has found that breeding females quickly learn to recognize the same person at a distance of about 20 m, especially when the nest is regularly visited, and give the alarm call. When other people approach the nest site (and may be unaware of its presence), however, they are greeted with silence. This demonstrates the level of variability in the birds' response to an intruder.

Eliot Howard records that later in the season, should any common enemy approach too closely, the female is 'most pugnacious during this period' (when the young are out of the nest and still dependent on her for food, and for the entire time that they are under her care). He cites the following instance of her pugnacity. 'When watching her on one occasion feeding her young, who were quite able to fly and thus escape any ordinary danger, I saw a Mistle Thrush settle on a very tall elm tree some distance away and commence to jerk his tail and chatter in a perfectly harmless manner, evidently with no evil intentions. He did not seem even to be aware of the presence of the Chiffchaff and her family who, however, appeared to resent his proximity, for, leaving the bushes, she flew straight up like a rocket to the top of the elm, and attacked the Mistle Thrush so vigorously that he at last flew away, pursued for some distance by the irate mother.'

Other observers have noted females carrying out distraction or luring displays when young in the nest have been approached or examined, some of these consisting of disablement-type actions similar to the broken-wing lure of a number of waders. In the main, this seems to involve running or hopping along the ground away from the nearby intruder accompanied by sharp 'tick' or 'djuck' notes. Homann in his extensive studies also recorded several instances of females leading (or attempting to lead, depending on age and mobility) the nestlings or fledglings away from the source of danger while persistently giving the sharp 'hooeet' note.

Preening and other comfort actions

In addition to the above range of behaviour, Chiffchaffs have a more private side to their lives, one shared by all birds, when they are indulging in quiet periods of rest or general inactivity, usually following periods of feeding or prolonged flights when moving long distances. At such times the individual may just sit quietly observing all that goes on around, perhaps from time to time indulging in some preening. At least once in the day a full preen will be carried out. Towards the moult period preening becomes even more important, and during the post-breeding moult the bird will become especially dowdy and (in anthropomorphic terms) rather morose and quiet, shunning a lot of activity and preferring the shady depths of bushes and well-leafed trees, venturing forth to feed only for short periods.

Chiffchaffs are, along with most other birds so far as we know, generally very healthy, and clearly have to be to stay alive. As part of the preening routine, they will often droop their wings and raise the leg on the same side of the body, through the gap between the wing and body, to shoulder level and then scratch by fast or vigorous movements of the foot the back of the head, the nape or more frequently the ear-coverts; to scratch further forward, around the forehead or the eye, the wing is held in a similar position but drooped slightly lower and the foot raised to the partially lowered head. This movement often involves the partial closing of the opaque nictitating membrane that covers the eye. This scratching is not necessarily always to remove parasites, although we know very little about the numbers of birds (of any species) which are totally unaffected by some kind of external parasite, but may be another kind of comfort movement, as some birds appear to gain some enjoyment from the activity.

At least once a day in hot regions or in the northern summer, an individual will bathe in a pool, puddle or at the edge of a large area of water provided it is clean and still. The bird stands up to its thighs and dips its belly feathers before splashing from side to side to flick up the water with its wings and bill. Following the bath, another comfort activity involves retreating to the lower branches of a convenient bush or shrub and, on a sheltered but laterally exposed perch, to dry and preen itself at the same time. This usually involves a considerable amount of wing-shaking or shuffling and vigorous shakes of the body and head to get rid of the excess water. This may be followed by periods of inactivity while the feathers are drying, or is interspersed with periods of much systematic rubbing of the feathers of certain parts of the wings, tail or body before moving on to the next area and nibbling wrongly placed feathers back into their correct position. When first emerging from its bath, the bird may be unrecognizable; it is only as it dries that the colour of the plumage returns.

Most preening activity follows bathing and oiling as part of the full daily clean-up and regulation of the plumage, but to a lesser extent it is also undertaken prior to roosting for the night. This may involve only a rudimentary preen, the fuller version having been undertaken earlier in the day, most likely during the midday to mid-afternoon lull in activity. It may be performed while sitting somewhere warm and sheltered or following a period of sunbathing. In the latter activity, carried out while stretched out on a perch or on the ground, the body feathers are ruffled up, the wings drooped and the tail spread to gain the maximum amount of warmth. This is most often undertaken on warm sunny days, often in autumn, particularly following periods of cold or wet weather.

Roosting

Depending on the time of year and the temperature, Chiffchaffs usually prepare to go to roost well before the onset of true dusk. They are generally not late singers, and most have retired from singing, even at the height of the courtship period, well before Willow Warblers have. Sites most

A Chiffchaff of the race canariensis resident on the western Canary Islands. It is similar to nominate race birds, but has duller upperparts, brighter yellow tones to the underparts and a slightly longer bill.

frequently chosen for roosting are well-concealed areas of fairly thick vegetation and the depths of leafy trees; bushes such as brambles, ivy or hawthorns are favoured spots, since they are able to provide shelter and relative safety from predators. In winter in Europe, Chiffchaffs have been recorded roosting in reedbeds, and a communal roost of up to 40 was watched entering a wood in Devon in the late afternoon of a dark December day. In southern Germany, one bird roosted for several nights in mid-winter in a bramble patch on a riverbank open to light, noise and wind; another exceptional record involved several birds which roosted inside a building on the Balearics where they had previously been seen when cold weather had set in.

When at roost, the bird is usually on a branch and the body feathers are fluffed out to allow maximum insulation and retention of the body heat. The head is either hunched down into the neck and shoulders or turned over the shoulder and the bill inserted between the scapular feathers. The toes curl around the perch (assisted by the padded texture of the soles of the feet) to grip it tightly in a kind of locking mechanism, which automatically tightens as the muscles of the thighs and leg relax. Deep sleep may not be maintained for any great length of time as in higher animals, but may be a series of cat-naps in which the individual periodically wakes to check that the surroundings are still safe and have not changed from the last check, albeit only a few minutes ago. Some birds may have short sleeps during the day, when the main period of feeding is over; these afternoon nap periods increase with the season and during the quiet or unobtrusive time of the post-breeding moult the Chiffchaff spends considerably more time napping or sleeping than at any other time of the year.

9

TERRITORY AND COURTSHIP

Establishing the territory

The behaviour of breeding Chiffchaffs on territory has been widely studied both in Britain and in central and eastern Europe. The establishment and defence of the territory involves males in considerable disputes and battles over the exact borders of the area of occupation. Most breeding territories are established within a week of the birds arriving back in the breeding area, and in areas of prime habitat most are soon occupied by singing males awaiting the arrival of the females.

It is important to define the differences in the two types of territory held and occupied. Firstly, that which is so strictly guarded and fought over by the male is the breeding territory, and within this area he is the master and no other male Chiffchaff may encroach without expecting either to be pursued out of it or challenged for domination of it, or part of it. The second and much larger area of territory, within which the breeding territory is situated, is the area in which the birds feed and possibly gather some of their nesting materials. The breeding territory is usually a relatively small area of up to 20 m in radius from the nest, while the larger area is perhaps better called a home range. In some cases such home ranges have been found, by ringing the birds holding territories within it, to cover fairly extensive areas: in one particular study area in an oak forest near Bourgogne in France, the average home range was approximately 9.9 ha, ie, an area 12 times the size of the average breeding territory.

These home ranges are best expressed as areas in which the birds are able to have a mutually agreed right of way in order to forage and feed. They may (depending on the habitat and density of breeding birds) be partly or wholly taken up by smaller breeding territories of other pairs, in which pursuits and challenges from resident males can be expected. It also seems likely that the female, because of her need to feed the brood, has a much wider home-range area than the male, which is likely to be pursued from occupied territories. In areas of particularly high breeding territory density most of the home range will be taken up and the territories will be continuous or, in some cases, even overlap slightly (by 2.6 per cent at a study site in central Norway). Since the Chiffchaff is usually extremely territorial and aggressive in defence of his area, such instances as this are somewhat unique and presumably the males are either in agreement about the boundary or spend most of the spring and summer in continual dispute over the limits of each other's territory.

Territory size is clearly linked to the availability of the habitat and the numbers of males competing for breeding territory within it. Studies reveal that the size of the breeding territory varies considerably, from 0.1-0.3 ha at a Welsh study site, 0.2-0.3 ha in Moscow region to 0.7 ha in Poland and 1 ha or more in Switzerland. In one particular study in central Norway, Saether (1983) found, from detailed observations of a number of pairs, that the average breeding territory measured 2258 m^2; this was calculated from a little over 20 territories which ranged from 491 m^2 at the smallest end to 4063 m^2 at the largest end of the range.

Eliot Howard again has a good and concise word on the establishment of the breeding territory. The 'demarcation of their [breeding] territory is best seen in long, narrow, wooded banks, which are inhabited by different males; here the boundaries can be watched with greater ease. In some cases it is almost possible to draw an imaginary line, across which neither male, whose territories are adjoining, will trespass; in other cases there is a small intervening space between the two territories, which again is not hunted by either male. 'In every case I have found these boundaries adhered to with the most amazing precision. Each male also appears to have some suitable position in his territory – a dead tree or perhaps a prominent larch – which he uses as his headquarters, and from which he makes little excursions into the different parts of his territory, always however, returning sooner or later to this central position.'

Breeding territories are both advertised and defended by males from the top of this prominently situated vantage point usually near to the centre of the territory. The defence of the territory is central to the success of attracting a female and rearing a brood. Some males, again depending on the state of stimulation and excitement, are much more territorial and aggressive than others and attack not only any intruding Chiffchaffs that arrive within (or near) the boundaries of the territory but also other migrants or resident birds such as Blue Tits. Attacks in defence of the territory usually consist of the threat display of wing-shivering, bill-snapping and tail-wagging together with a loud burst of antagonistic song, which is really just a loud or prolonged version of the typical song. Actual physical attacks or the striking of an intruder in the defence of a territory are not particularly commonplace but may happen more often than the current observations suggest. Once the intruder moves or flies from his initial position on being discovered, the occupying male gives chase until the intruder is safely escorted to the edge of the territory and ejected. These chases are often interrupted for varying reasons, mostly depending on the reluctance of the intruder to be ejected and seek new territory elsewhere or its desire to dispute the initial title-holder's claim. For later-arriving birds continual ejection from one territory to another may be somewhat problematic, since the area into which he has been ejected may well (particularly in areas of high density) be another Chiffchaff's territory and the whole process begins anew, unless he is fortunate to be able to find an as yet unoccupied territory. The removal of intruding males by existing territory-holders begins from the moment the territory is established and reaches a peak during the period of greatest competition with other males, with the main arrival of females, declining in intensity only following the period of pair-formation and copulation.

In those cases where fights do occur as a result of an intruder staying his ground, these usually consist of birds attempting to chase each other off the territory and aerial clashes follow on from the chase. These fights are somewhat reminiscent of male House Sparrows seeking dominance over each other (although with less excited noise and without several hangers-on) in that the chase can last for some time, with one bird pursuing and then being pursued and with occasional bursts of loud antagonistic song from whichever bird considers himself the rightful owner. When the two birds meet head-on in mid-air, fights ensue in which they lock claws and tumble to the ground with wings extended; once on the ground, the fight usually ends and the birds separate and retreat to more normal perches.

In not all cases, however, are the results of these contests or tussles so peacefully settled, since they may sometimes be followed by bursts of loud song or song-duels where the individuals attempt to enforce their claim to the territory by outsinging each other. Song-duels are more typically recorded in the early part of the breeding season, when territories are being defended over a wide area of suitable habitat; such bursts of loud or antagonistic singing are directed from at close range, approximately 1–2m, at encroaching males.

Disputes are particularly common along the borders of territories in areas of high density. In such cases there are frequent incursions into each other's territory, both knowingly and unwittingly, which provoke threats and chases. Such disputes may sometimes last for a considerable period of time, in one case up to three or four hours. Threats in the form of wing-shivering and bill-clicking by the territory-holder are given some emphasis when pursuing an intruder by the rattle or 'trr-rr' call, which may be uttered repeatedly or as part of the loud antagonistic song. Eliot Howard gives a particularly good account of the way in which two males on adjoining territories attempt to establish the territory border 'as they work their way towards the same boundary simultaneously. As they approach the boundary the song becomes more frequent and very hurried, their whole attitude being one of great excitement. As they approach still more closely, this excitement increases, their wings are jerked about, the song deteriorates into a few notes rapidly uttered, they still pretend to hunt for food in a half-hearted sort of manner, but all the time it is evident that each one is keeping a close watch on the other's movements: then the climax is reached, they dart at one another, tumbling over and over in the air, their bills clicking loudly; and then their honour appearing to be satisfied, they immediately retire to their respective territories'. In such disputes over the establishment of territory, the ensuing chases may involve pursuit not only out of the area of the territory of the holder but also through those of neighbouring males, who also give chase in turn, resulting in several birds giving chase.

In areas of high density territorial disputes are a frequent activity and part of the daily routine for the males, since it is highly likely that they come into regular contact with each other when patrolling the limits of

A tristis Chiffchaff wintering in Lincolnshire. The edges to the primaries show a dull green edge in early spring.

their breeding territories. Eliot Howard noted from his extensive studies of the bird that 'as the weeks pass by these combats become so frequent, occurring again and again during the same morning, that I am inclined to think that they are prompted largely by a love of play. If this is the case, and they are games only, then they are exceptionally vigorous ones, differing only in their duration from the fights which take place earlier in the season over the possession of the breeding territory.' In one area of south-west England nests have been recorded less than 40 m apart, while in northern Spain singing males advertised their territories from songposts no more than 50 m apart in areas of mixed forest with bramble undergrowth, and in an oak forest in Germany they were more widely spaced at between 80 and 100 m.

Aggressive behaviour by female Chiffchaffs is rare, except in such instances given above where she is in defence of the nest or young or in exceptional cases where two females are paired with the same male. At such times she will defend the young against almost any birds of similar size and even drive off the male with vigorous pursuit. In one notable example H. G. Hurrell, the well-known Devon ornithologist and writer on birds and their habits, recorded a case of bigamy in which the two females drove off a third female which subsequently appeared within their territory.

There are a number of recorded instances of aggression being shown by Chiffchaffs, particularly males on territory, to Willow Warblers. In one case, a Chiffchaff in Scotland successfully defended its territory on three separate occasions against repeated intrusion by a Willow Warbler, the latter finally abandoning its attempt to oust the sitting tenant. Such instances seem, however, to be quite rare, since in many areas the two species co-exist in a kind of harmony. Garcia, who studied the territorial behaviour of both species in woods near Oxford, found that the two largely ignored each other and each species sang and fed in its own territory with no adverse effects on the other; pursuit flights and chases were rare, possibly stimulated by the presence of intruding Chiffchaffs in the general area, and were broken off when the Willow Warbler sang, suggesting that they were probably due to mistaken identity. Studies at sites in central Norway have shown that almost completely overlapping Chiffchaff and Willow Warbler territories occur; in a five-year period one site was occupied at times by up to three Willow Warblers and between three and six Chiffchaff territories.

Pair-formation: courtship and display

Male Chiffchaffs return from their wintering areas on average about two to three weeks ahead of the females in some years of particularly bad or late winter weather the first returning birds have not been seen until the first few days of April. The territory is established and defended by the male, who advertises his presence from a number of prominent songposts; the size of the initial territory may expand, particularly where there are no other Chiffchaffs to dispute the boundaries, or it may contract when new arrivals move in and assume dominance over part of the area. The size of the territory is dependent on what size area of the habitat is likely to be viable to support the immediate requirements of the breeding pair and the young, while this has to be balanced against what size area can be defended by the male.

Following the establishment of the territory the male announces his presence and the territory to any females by singing a loud and repeated song. A large part of his daily cycle is taken with up with frequent searches of the area at canopy level (where most singing is done), but an increasing amount of time is also spent at lower levels in the wood where any passing female is more likely to be present. Females occupy a much more terrestrial range of habitats than the males; for most of the breeding season they keep primarily to the ground and scrub layers of vegetation, only occasionally venturing up into the upper tree levels for feeding, copulation and when taking the young away from the nest.

As the spring progresses, the male shows a restless urge to find a mate and consequently spends less time singing in the canopy level and more time searching for a female by uttering a plaintive contact note. It is generally thought that males recognize females by their habit of feeding at low levels (at this time of year, males would be competing with others for territories), their lack of aggressive response to the male and their long drawn-out 'hweet' contact note; females also, of course, do not compete with the males by singing. At the first meeting of the two, the male greets the female with a close but not particularly purposeful dive-bombing attack. The female may evade this or she may take flight, at which the male follows and a chase ensues. If during the course of the chase she strays out of the territory into that of the next male, the latter will also join in the pursuit. If the female remains within the first territory, the male keeps close company with her and frequently pursues her through the territory often while uttering a loud burst of song as part of the excitement as a prelude to the formation of the pair. On contact, the birds click their bills at each other.

During the period of pair-formation the male increasingly performs a courtship flight and elaborately floats slowly down to the female on outspread butterfly-like wings. These courtship flights, which are frequently repeated and may extend over a period of a few days, are either direct or spiralling, and involve slow and deliberate wing-flapping as the bird takes off, to descend slowly on outspread wings with tail slightly raised and partly fanned and with legs dangling. The formation of the pair-bond is completed shortly after this, when the male ceases his advertisement song and will drive other females out of the territory. Both sexes spend an increasing time at low levels in the territory and the male follows the female when the two are foraging low down or on the ground; the male occasionally utters a burst of song from a low perch while she is on the

Various display postures of excitement adopted by male Chiffchaffs when singing to attract a female.

The watching posture adopted by the male Chiffchaff following pair-formation and when the female is within the territory selected the nest site.

---

ground and presumably searching for a nest site. At this time he also adopts a characteristic posture from a low branch or similar vantage point to watch the female while she is on the ground; in this watching posture the head is held down and forwards with the body slightly hunched (the crown, mantle and back feathers partially raised) and at a slight angle, the throat and breast feathers are puffed out, the wings are slightly open and drooped, and the tail is held pressed down and fanned. Occasionally the tail is slowly but rather stiffly swivelled from side to side. The female shows little or no obvious response to the courtship flight of the male, but some have been known to open their gape and hold the head forwards, slightly hunched or to sleek down the plumage, which may be a prelude to mating.

The courtship and the slightly slower excitement songs of the male increase in frequency and pitch during the chases and often include vigorous wing-flapping or wing-waving (either one wing or the other). At intervals of particular intensity between the two, the male may flick both wings alternately (almost as intensely or as excitedly as a displaying Dunnock) and perform repeated bill-snapping in playful or mock-attack fashion at the female as part of the display.

At close encounters between the two, either on the ground or on a low-level perch, both birds flick their wings vigorously at each other. At more intimate times, they slightly shiver their wings, particularly the female as part of the submission stage of the courtship. She also utters a sharp 'hooeet' or abrupt 'dik' notes, the male giving a rattling 'trr' or 'r-rr'.

Within days of formating the pair the nest site is chosen and construction begins. Copulation first occurs during the initial stages. This can be as the conclusion to an excited low-level chase with both birds tumbling over and over and ending up on the ground, or the two approach each other on a low branch with wings slightly drooped and shivering (this may follow a period of loud and rapid singing by the male). The female raises her tail, which is slowly opened and fanned, and gives a short series of 'it-it' or 'drit' notes or more feeble and thin 'siff-siff' or 'tsif-tsif' notes as a soliciting call while approaching the male. When close to the male, the latter mounts her for brief copulation before flying off, occasionally in courtship or butterfly display fight, to sing or respond to the female (who may still be calling the plaintive soliciting note) with a short or rather sharp 'drit'.

Following such incidents or playful periods of courtship, particularly early in the morning, the female is clearly receptive to the male, as shown by the quivering wings and generally submissive posture with lowered head and raised tail. The actual coupling of the pair is fairly brief and lasts only a matter of seconds, although the act of copulation may be repeated several times during the course of several hours. Its timing is determined entirely by the female, who will respond to the male with the soliciting call to show her willingness and that she is in the peak of condition for mating. From a perch close to the female, the male moves to her side while she is almost horizontal across the perch with her head held slightly lower than the rest of her body; her tail is partially raised (revealing the undertail-coverts and vent) and the wings slightly drooped and all the time she utters a thin and rather piping soliciting call. The male hovers briefly over her back before landing gently, and then proceeds to adopt the same position with his head down and body held horizontal whilst pressing down on her. He holds his wings out to cover the female and for balance while she fully raises her tail at an angle slightly above 45°, allowing him access to her sex organs; with tail held down he makes contact with her and in the space of very few seconds the minute drops of semen are transferred.

Studies carried out over a period of many years at Bookham Common

The intensity of the courtship song by the male is often accompanied by vigorous wing-flapping or waving of either one or both of the wings.

The display-flight of a male Chiffchaff. On fully outspread flat wings he spirals round and down to the female.

in Surrey by Geoffrey Beven show that there are slight variations to the copulation ritual. Some copulations may be performed on the ground or low down in a bush. In some cases, a female has been recorded jumping about in a tree giving the soliciting call and slowly flicking her wings; the approaching male responded with a similar call and held his wings out, shivering slightly, held his head and tail low and fanned his tail. At the sight of this the female moved towards him and he mounted her.

It is possible to see both sexes together at any time of the day (brief periods of courtship and display have been noted on warm fine evenings), but the most intense period for full display and copulation is, as with many other bird species, early morning. This period of copulation and intimacy as part of the pair-bonding is relatively short-lived, and at no other time in the year do the birds touch or come into contact with each other.

The formation of the pair lasts for the duration of the breeding season, which for some Chiffchaffs of the nominate and northern races may be two months. Even in cases where both partners return to the same breeding site in following years, there is little recognition or fidelity between the two. The male's involvement is at its greatest from pair-formation and courtship to egg-laying, declining once the eggs have been laid. Despite active observation of the female and perhaps the progress of the brood and defence of the territory, there is little active contribution from the male and his role declines to zero throughout the feeding of the brood. Where there are second broods the bond is maintained, but again only for a short period. Some females frequently show aggression towards the male, which they clearly regard as an interloper in the proceedings of raising the young.

10

BREEDING BEHAVIOUR

Within days of the formation of the pair, mating will have taken place and the female will have selected the nest site. This can be either towards the centre or at the edge of the territory; in the study site at Wytham Woods in Oxfordshire, the majority were at the edge of the territory. The chief consideration given by the female to the choice of nest site is the amount of concealment afforded. One of the commonest locations is within a thick bramble bush or a tangle of nettles and overgrown vegetation in the understorey layer.

The nest (of any of the races) is usually built at a height of within 1 m of the ground, but it can be either on the ground or placed so low down that there is only the barest amount of room beneath it. In central Europe, Schönfeld reported (1980) that of 80 nests studied in detail 31 per cent were on the ground, 51 per cent were up to 30 cm from the ground, 14 per cent were between 31–50 cm from the ground and the remaining 4 per cent were over 51 cm above the ground. Elsewhere in Europe there are exceptional records of Chiffchaffs nesting at up to 1.2 m and 2.4 m from the ground.

Nests on the ground are more common for first broods as the vegetation cover is much more sparse, certainly for the northern breeding birds, than when nests for second or replacement clutches are built. There is some evidence to suggest that nests built at higher elevations are a response to particular predators, such as rats or stoats, which have become used to preying on low-nesting birds. A study of breeding birds in the Moscow region showed that Chiffchaffs that bred at the usual level – on or just above the ground – were invariably unsuccessful, with the nests being robbed by a predator, whereas those that built at between 2.6 and 4.3 m were successful. Further north, on the Yamal peninsula, Russian researchers found that the average height of 19 nests was 1.9 m from the ground; one, 11 m up, was the highest ever recorded.

Over much of western Europe and the British Isles, the earliest returning Chiffchaffs start nest-building in April, but those which have moved further south for the winter and take longer to return begin breeding up to a month later. Thus, nest construction throughout the range of *collybita* and *abietinus* can be found throughout most of April and early to mid-May. The timing is much the same for *tristis*, except that those breeding in the tundra and the edge of forest areas at the most northerly outposts of the range do not commence nest-building until early June. At the opposite end of the range, birds of the race *canariensis* are nest-building at the turn of the year, as Bannerman (1963) records several nests with eggs in early February, although the main period here seems to be from late February to June, with birds at the coast laying earlier than those at higher altitudes; there are also several records of birds feeding young at the nest in July, so the breeding period in this race is particularly extended.

Nest construction

The nest is built by the female. There are records of the male assisting in one or two isolated instances, but only very occasionally, perhaps during the latter stages. The construction is usually completed within 4-10 days, depending on the state of the female. Nest-building begins in the early morning and, apart from a short pause around midday, lasts throughout the day, especially in damp or wet weather when the plant material is easily shaped. Once the site is chosen, the female completes a lower layer of rough material, such as leaves, grass or plant stems, and creates a small depression by constant turning and settling movements. After a secure base has been established the nest floor is built, and then the rest of the nest over the following two or three days. Collection and construction of the lining is completed in the final two days. The female's energy, drive and ability to gather, in anything up to 1500 separate flights, so many hundreds or thousands of different pieces of nesting material in such a short space of time have to be admired. In addition to collecting the materials, she must also bind them together meticulously.

The construction of the nest marks the beginning of the end of the male's involvement in the proceedings; from now on he is at best a disinterested spectator who is on hand to offer only occasional assistance

A female Chiffchaff collecting nesting material from the ground, usually this is solely the female's job.

and to maintain the defence of the territory. The female is responsible for incubation and caring for the young. In general the male takes little or no notice of her activities and can be more of a hindrance than a help, making playful attacks or dive-bombing runs at her while she is gathering nesting material. Some males, especially in the early part of nest-building, keep a close watch on the female and either infrequently call with the 'hooeet' contact note or give short bursts of song. When the female is incubating, she is frequently pursued by the male when she leaves the nest; almost as if he is chivvying her to return to her chore of building the nest.

Material for the nest is gathered from a wide area, usually within the territory, but there are records of birds collecting up to 120 m from the site of the nest. I cannot improve on the description of the nest given by Eliot Howard: 'The nest is an exceedingly pretty one, dome-shaped, with the entrance at one side rather than near the top; the outside is composed of dead leaves, chiefly mixed with some of the coarser dead grasses; next to this dead grass forms the principal material mixed with fine roots; next to this, again is the lining, which is composed of feathers only; but it seems that close to the lining finer and more delicate grasses are used than those on the outer parts. The lower portion of the nest is more stoutly built than the upper, and the dead leaves are more securely glued together.' Further materials noted by other authors have included small plant stems, fine stalks, horse hair, poplar down and moss, the latter two in particular as an addition to or an alternative to feathers for the lining. In the case of the pair mentioned above, which bred under the eaves of a cottage on Gran Canaria, Bannerman (1963) records that the birds 'made free use of large pieces of cotton wool which were placed for them.' Chiffchaffs appear to use dead leaves as part of the nest foundation more frequently than do Willow Warblers. The latter species, whose nests are very similar in size and shape, but more often placed on the ground, seems to have a preference for coarse grasses and honeysuckle bark as a material for the base.

Dimensions of Chiffchaff nests vary and may reflect the age of the female and whether she has constructed a nest before. In the British Isles most nests are about 12.5 cm high and about 11cm wide; elsewhere in Europe, nests of between 8 and 15 cm in height and 8 and 13 cm in width have also been recorded. Nests constructed for the second brood are often slightly larger and heavier, presumably because more material is available at that time of the year. The thickness of the nest wall is usually a minimum of 2–2.5 cm and can be up to as much as 4 cm deep. The entrance hole is usually just wide enough to allow the adults access to tend and feed the young, throughout much of the breeding range in Britain and northern Europe this measures on average between 3.5 and 4 cm across, and elsewhere entrances of up to 5 cm have been found. However, constant use of the entrance by the adult female feeding the young together with the increasing size of the nestlings will, to a certain degree, change or extend the shape of the entrance hole, and measurements of old or recently deserted nests may be larger than the dimensions given here.

Across the entire range, the shape and general dimensions of the nest seem to be exact, and there are very few variations on record from this design. Almost the only exception is the record by W. H. Dobie of a nest in Cheshire in June 1932 built in a berberis bush: this was cup-shaped without a domed covering – the leaves of the bush formed a perfect umbrella over the nest. It was successful and several young fledged from it.

If the female is disturbed during the early stages of construction, she will abandon the site and move to another; material from the old site may also be taken and moved to the new site. At one site in Germany, a female was recorded building two nests simultaneously at two different sites (Geissbühler 1954), while the male watched the construction of both with occasional encouraging bursts of song. Several other authors have reported that the female, while gathering nesting material, becomes almost oblivious of human presence and will tolerate very close approach.

Breeding Chiffchaffs may not always be obvious, and detailed surveys of territory establishment require many hours of constant effort, particularly in the early morning when most activity and song is likely. The nest of the Willow Warbler, by way of comparison, is almost always on the ground, in a small depression, frequently on a bank or similar sloping area, and concealed by a clump of grass or other vegetation and with the entrance similarly disguised.

Eggs

Within a day of the nest being completed the first egg is laid, and thereafter a single egg is laid daily until the clutch is complete. Depending on the region and the race included, this may be (for *collybita*, *abietinus* and *tristis*) from the middle of April to early July or, exceptionally, to the end of July. In Ireland, there is an unusual record of a clutch being laid as late as 13 and 14 August. Southern Chiffchaffs, particularly *canariensis* can have complete clutches from the beginning of February, and even occasionally from the end of January. Except in the case of the most northerly breeders, eggs laid from early June onwards are more likely to be second clutches.

The eggs are small and slightly more oval than rounded, usually described as subelliptical. They have a slightly glossy, creamy-white base colour on which there is a varying amount of sparsely distributed, tiny, dark red, reddish-brown, purple or blackish spots, which are confined mostly to the broader end of the egg but can cover the whole surface; in somewhat rarer instances, the eggs can be entirely unmarked. Those eggs on which the spots cover the whole area are generally similar to Willow Warbler eggs, but the latter have paler brown spots (and are usually more densely covered with finer dots and spots). The eggs measure on average 15.3 mm at the longest point and about 12.1 mm wide, extremes of these measurements (from a range of 318 eggs measured) being from 12.3 to 17.7 mm in length and 10.7 to 13.7 mm in width. They average 1.21g in width, ranging from 1 to 1.41g.

The usual clutch of Chiffchaffs of the races *collybita*, *abietinus* and *tristis* is five or six eggs, but others of between two and seven are not unknown and clutches of three and four are fairly usual in parts of eastern Europe and Scandinavia. Extreme clutches of one (if, indeed, one egg can be said to constitute a clutch) and nine have also been recorded. The usual clutch of *canariensis* is four eggs. If any eggs are lost through the nest being robbed by a predator, replacements will be laid within a day or so of the loss, provided the season is not too far advanced. Replacement clutches or

A full clutch seen through the entrance to the domed nest.

An adult female Chiffchaff (of the race collybita) *at the entrance to the nest.*

second layings generally contain fewer eggs than those laid previously: of 34 recorded first clutches the number of eggs averaged between five and six eggs, which dropped to between four and five in second or subsequent clutches; in a replacement of the second clutch, the number of eggs dropped again to between three and four.

Incubation

The completion of the clutch marks the beginning of the incubation period. Over most of the southern and central parts of the range this lasts for 13 – 15 days, starting from the time the last, or in some cases the penultimate, egg was laid. Incubation is undertaken solely by the female, who sits, during daylight hours, for up to 40 minutes at a time before taking breaks of between five and fifteen minutes to feed. During the first days she takes only short and relatively infrequent breaks, usually early in the morning, but as the period progresses the breaks become longer and more frequent. During this time the male has no contact with the nest but often approaches and gives the 'hooeet' call; in the main he is busy looking after the defence of the territory, but he also spends some time singing from a perch close to, if not actually over, the nest. When the female departs from the nest she does so quickly and silently, flying a few feet before uttering her contact note. During this time the two parents have often been found feeding together, the male accompanying the female on the return to the nest. As with her departure from the nest, her return to it is silent.

Nestling development

The eggs hatch over a period of up to two days. The shells are removed from the nest by the female, who is careful not to reveal the whereabouts of the nest to any potential predator. For the first days of life the tiny young are naked, with pinkish-red skin, and their eyes are closed. Feeding begins almost immediately and, following feeding, the female broods the young for periods of up to ten minutes at a time during the daylight hours, before dashing off to collect food. The whole brood, or only one or two of the young, may be fed once or twice during her feeding stints before she resumes her brooding position. Eliot Howard, who devoted considerable time to recording the nesting behaviour of the British warblers, stated that the actual time of 12 minutes spent brooding the offspring was 'adhered to with remarkable accuracy, varying only a minute one way or the other', as if the bird too, had a stop watch to set her visits by. As the amount of food brought to the nest for the young increases over the first seven or eight days, the amount of time spent brooding the nestlings decreases. The young are brooded at night until about the ninth or tenth day.

When brooding the nestlings the female utters a quiet purring note, audible only from a metre or so. This note, which is also given just prior to leaving the nest, may act as an individual recognition call for the nestlings. The 'hooeet' call is also given frequently by some females (but considerable variation exists between pairs and areas) as a contact note call to the male, and especially when returning to the nest (as opposed to when leaving it silently). At this stage the male, whose role it seems has been merely to accompany the female and occasionally regale her with a short refrain, sings while the female is brooding the nestlings, and also apparently (for those males that do) when carrying food.

The feeding of the nestlings is mostly the work and responsibility of the female, and observations have shown that she needs to bring in a minimum of 200-220 items of food every day for up to 12 days to sustain their growth rates. This may involve her bringing in more than one item at a time, which in turn requires extra foraging before she has enough to satisfy the demands of the nestlings.

Although, as with most other parental activities, the male takes little or no active part in brood-feeding, there are a number of instances where males have been recorded bringing food to the young in the nest. Even in the cases where males do participate in feeding the young, they rarely contribute more than 25 per cent of the effort by the female, especially for first broods. This may consist merely of escorting the female to and from the nest as she forages and collects small insects and their larvae, or he may act as a lookout and give the alarm note, which seems to be his main function, at the approach of a predator or actively bring food for part of the time when the young are in the nest. One male at a study site in south-west England participated in the feeding of the young for the first four or five days following hatching, while researchers elsewhere have noted males taking an active role only from about the seventh or eighth day. In particularly wet weather or at other periods when there is a risk that the female may not be able to find sufficient food for the young, he may help. In studies of the breeding behaviour of Chiffchaffs at a site in Germany, Treuenfels reported that one male's share of the feeding of the nestlings was equal to about one-third of that of the female. In cases where the female had suddenly disappeared, the male took over the feeding of the

A female Chiffchaff brings food to her nestlings.

young, but it seems that he may not be able to sustain this or find sufficient food to rear the young to fledging.

In those cases where both parents are tending and feeding the young, the male usually has dominance over the female who waits for him to depart before flying to the nest; the reverse is not always true, however, and the male will arrive at the nest while the female is feeding or brooding the young. At one site being watched by Treuenfels (1940), the female took the food brought to the nest by the male and fed it to the young. Males and females which are tending the same nest are said by some authors to have separate feeding areas but this seems to be in isolated areas for there are a number of recent records where both collected food from the same source.

The rate of growth of the nestlings is clearly related to and dependent on the amount of food they are given, but on average between days five and nine they grow extremely rapidly, putting on as much as 1000 mg every day. Following this period of high consumption the level of feeding and growth decelerates and by the time the young are ready to leave the nest they will have received sufficient to increase their weight by between 50 and 150 mg. Thus, their weight on leaving the nest will be in the region of about 8.1–8.9 g, which is approximately the weight of the adults.

The diet of the nestlings is of softer food items than that of the adults and fledglings, with more larval and aphid content. The species and amount of insects that comprise their diet seem to vary with locality, season and weather. Studies in Europe and Asia have shown that a high proportion is made up of Lepidoptera, Diptera, small molluscs, stoneflies, spiders and lacewings, supplemented by aphids, larval beetles and caterpillars when available; in one particular location in Moldavia, the young were at one stage in their development fed solely on the abundant larvae of one of the *Tortrix* moths, the adults bringing in up to 4–6 caterpillars at a time. Large caterpillars are brought to the nest and beaten from side to side against a branch before being fed to the nestlings. Adult insects which have a chitinous shell are crushed in the bill or beaten against a branch to remove the shell. Some of the larger items are broken into more manageable fragments by the female before being offered to the young.

The cleanliness of the nest appears to be the responsibility of the female, who, in the early days of feeding the nestlings, swallows the faecal sacs as they are produced by the young shortly after being fed. After several days she then removes them in her bill to a nearby branch, or she may discard them in flight over a random area roughly 7–12 m from the nest; one study found that, in a period of 16–17 hours of daylight, she removed between 50 and 55 faecal sacs from the nest.

The chicks acquire a short and somewhat sparse growth of long dark grey down on the head, particularly over the eyes, and more sparsely on the upperparts during their first few days of life. Their eyes open gradually during the sixth and seventh days, and between then and fledging the juvenile plumage is fairly rapidly acquired. This begins as rows of feather quills or pins, particularly along the wings and the tail, from which the feathers sprout at the top; elsewhere on the body the quills are more widely separated and begin as tufts of loosely growing feathers. The feathers grow fairly rapidly, and the nestlings soon become covered in brownish body feathers and dark mossy-green on the wings and tail, although the feathers are still for the most part spiky and seemingly loose-fitting so that the birds

Nestlings at about 12 days, almost ready to leave the nest.

An adult female Chiffchaff brings food to the nest as the young grow rapidly in their first two weeks of life.

resemble little feathered balls with pinkish heads (the last area to become well feathered) and bright yellow gapes.

Shortly after their twelfth day, usually between the 14th and 15th days, but possibly slightly earlier if they are disturbed or forced to by a predator, the young venture out of the nest and are able to make short and clumsy or ungainly flights of about 5–10 metres. This results in the brood quickly becoming dispersed over a wide area around the immediate vicinity of the nest, but although they are mostly hidden within the ground or low growth they give loud contact calls.

The fledged young remain within the general area of the nest for most of their developing period, which may be as long as three or four weeks, and in the early days of leaving the nest utter a contact note to keep in touch with each other and to let the adult female, returning with food, know their whereabouts. On first fledging the young are unable to fend for or feed themselves and are still heavily dependent on the adult, usually the female, for sustenance. Fledglings which have lost contact with the rest of the brood give a constant call which soon descends into a 'sweep' or a more melancholy 'weep' note. It is the adult female who keeps the family together and decides if the brood should move and where they will roost.

As the adult gets near, the young give food-begging calls while gaping in nestling fashion for food. These begging calls depend on whether the individual can see the female or is alerted to her presence by her contact note. if the young bird is unable to see her, the contact call is continued. Young birds that are in the presence of the female with food utter a dry or whispering note especially if two or more are gathered together on the same branch while huddling up to the adult bird; if the female comes to feed a fledgling which is not gaping, the food is pushed against the side of the bill in an effort to make the youngster gape for food. The response of the young birds to the calls of the female is innately conditioned and developed at an early age: nestlings will crouch down in the nest with their heads drawn in, while fledglings freeze where they are, even on an open perch, and allow close approach until forced to take off at the last moment. fleeing in panic and giving the loud distress call.

Until the young are fully fledged and the brood has dispersed, the family remains within the home-range area of the territory, where there is a sufficiency of food available and the male will be on hand to alert the brood or defend them from predators. At night the male roosts close to the nest and from the laying of the first egg the female never leaves the nest at night until the young are fledged. Once out of the nest, the young roost together in low dense undergrowth or on an open branch, which may be several metres from the ground. The female will choose the roosting site and may return the young to the same site for successive nights; Homann (1960) recorded one family using the same roost site for up to 16 nights before moving 170 m to a different site. When sleeping, the young bunch closely together for warmth and fluff out their feathers while crouching down, balancing on their tarsi and breast bones on the branch; they may (towards the end of the period as a family unit) turn their heads over the shoulders, but most fledglings just draw their heads down into the neck.

As the days pass and the brood grows, the food-begging calls and the huddling behaviour towards the adult decrease; in the latter instances the female discourages the young from attempting to huddle up to her by flying off immediately they show signs of wanting physical contact. From about 14 days the broods show signs of breaking up and becoming more adventurous and independent, as they spend less time begging for food and

Newly-fledged Chiffchaffs await the arrival of food which will be brought to them by the female parent.

take an inquisitive interest in their surroundings. From about the 19th day the amount of food brought by the female declines to very little and may be sufficient to sustain the level of nourishment required by the individual. From 20–22 days the young are able to undertake fairly long flights on strengthening wings and actively seek out insects and other food items, but they still pursue the female when she arrives with food and youngsters have been seen being fed at 28 days of age. Studies of ringed birds at several sites in northern Russia have shown that within the first few weeks of independence there is no great urge to travel far from the natal area, and some individuals have been retrapped within 6–7 hectares of the breeding site up to a month later.

Towards the end of the breeding season in late summer, either within the territory or in an area of abundant feeding, the family party may become part of a larger group which may ultimately contain not only other Chiffchaff families but also those of other warblers, such as Whitethroats or Lesser Whitethroats, or possibly family parties of other birds such as Blue or Coal Tits. At such times the family members keep in touch with each other by the frequent use of the 'hooeet' contact note. During these late-summer days when there is an ample supply of insect food, these groups or family parties indulge in youthful play-acting and develop actions and responses they will need as adults. This involves the development of aggression by the use of mock-threats and posturing, and also the chasing off of other birds, whether related or not, which are seen as interlopers. This may be just be a simple display of aggression and threat to a Blue Tit that happens to come too close while feeding or the active pursuit in flight and through bushes and trees of another young Chiffchaff. On calm early-autumn days, it is often possible to watch parties or loose flocks of Chiffchaffs flycatching from trees and bushes in secluded or warm and sheltered spots. From time to time one will interrupt feeding to watch the actions of another and, judging his attack to the second, wait for the 'interloper' to launch after a passing insect before giving chase. The development of this aggression or posturing not only involves chases and the mock-pursuit of others, but also may be backed up with closer encounters involving gaping or bill-snapping and the sleeking of plumage.

The break-up of the family follows soon after the last of the brood becomes independent or the parents refuse to answer food-begging calls. The young drift off away from the rest of the family party, gradually moving further and further from the original nest site. The adult birds, depending on the time of year and length of the season, may either undertake similar movements away from the disused territory to undergo a post-breeding moult or begin a second brood.

Polygamy

There are only a small number of documented occurrences of polygamy by breeding Chiffchaffs, which, considering the amount of time the male has in which to do seemingly very little except sing and maintain the defence of the territory, is perhaps surprising. The factors which favour polygamy could be said to be tailor-made for species such as the Chiffchaff: a long breeding season, an ability to replace lost clutches (or broods), areas of high density in the population, the female undertaking most work in the incubation and care of the young and the male having little to do with the care of the offspring, tolerance of females within a polygamous relationship, and the ability of females to rear the young alone.

In most instances where polygamy has been recorded in Chiffchaffs, it is primarily (though not necessarily consistently) in areas of particularly high density. In one such area, the Bialowieza forest in eastern Poland, it was recorded in three of the four years that the study was undertaken. Results from this study showed that up to just over 22 per cent of the males present were polygamous, but in some years the level of polygamy was lower than in others, e.g. in one year only five of 179 territorial males only had two females. In most cases, and in the Bialowieza and the Wytham Woods studies, one male paired with two females, but in one case at both sites, one male paired with three females. It became clear that the first female arrived about three or four days ahead of the second, but the results do not show whether the first was aware of the second.

Other results of the study showed that some males may be monogamous for the duration of the first brood and polygamous for the second or, conversely, bigamous for the first brood and unpaired for the second-brood period. Also, the territory sizes of polygamous birds did not apparently differ from those of monogamous pairs. In Germany a monogamous male for the first brood took over the female of an adjoining pair as well as his female of the first brood for the second brood and defended both territories as an increased larger territory. The age of the females involved in polygamous relationships seems not to be an influencing factor, since both of those in Germany were at least two years old. At a second site in Germany, near Karlsruhe, Homann (1960) reported the case of a male which courted a female early in the season and then switched his attention to another, with whom he raised a brood, while another female, possibly the first bird, built a nest within a metre of the second female's nest after the brood had fledged.

In England, H. G. Hurrell noted an instance of possible polygamy in Devon when a male deserted his mated female at the egg-laying stage and her eggs failed. She then moved to an adjacent territory, about 180 m away, and helped to feed the offspring of the pair holding territory there. Both females subsequently re-laid, the first about 30 m from the site of the second, and the two subsequently became aggressive towards each other.

Within the *Phylloscopus* genus as a whole, polygamy is somewhat exceptional, but some members, such as Wood Warbler and more particularly Willow Warblers in some parts of their range, appear to be more prone to polygamous relationships. This is especially evident in areas or years where there is a natural excess of females over males. Studies of Wood Warblers in areas of central and northern Europe, where the population is high, have shown that incidences of polygamy vary between 30 and 40 per cent in some years while in others, perhaps cyclically, it may be quite rare. In a study of Willow Warblers in central Russia, an area containing up to 364 nests held mostly monogamously paired birds, but over three years the rate of polygamous relationships varied between 5 and 17 per cent of the population. A similar study of bird populations, carried out at Witley Common in Surrey over the period from 1977 to 1982, found that just over 13 per cent of a total of 136 male Willow Warblers were polygamous, the highest proportion in any single year being a quarter of the breeding population of 28 males. In both instances it appeared that the second female was 'acquired' after the first female had started incubating, i.e. about six days later, and that, although both females became aware of each other, no hostility was shown between them.

As in other cases where polygamy occurs, it is not because of an absence of males, since in many areas where the population is high there are more males than females. In a study of a Chiffchaff population in a wood in south-west England over 33 years, M. P. Price noted that, even in years when there was a high population (about 17 birds) as many as six males in a year could be unpaired.

Hybrids

There are a number of reports of hybridization between Chiffchaffs and Willow Warblers. Mostly involve individuals giving mixed songs or the song of the 'other' species, but for various reasons very few are actually confirmed as genuine hybrids. In one instance where hybridization was strongly suspected, in Lothian, Scotland, Chiffchaff and Willow Warbler males had taken up territory in overlapping areas. When a female Willow Warbler arrived, both males were aggressive towards each other. After a few days, the male Willow Warbler disappeared and was later presumed killed. Subsequently, the male Chiffchaff was later found helping the female Willow Warbler to rear a brood of seven young within his territory. The young were ringed, and one returned to the area two years later and gave a mixed song with phrases of both Chiffchaff and Willow Warbler. In addition to records of hybridization with Willow Warblers, four out of a total of 11 Chiffchaffs collected in Iranian Azerbaijan showed characters of being hybrids with Mountain Chiffchaff (Vaurie 1954).

Second broods

Throughout most of the northern parts of the range, there is sufficient time to raise only a single brood. In the central and southern parts of the range (north to southern and central England and east to at least the area between Moscow and St Petersburg, and in isolated instances further north in Scotland and Finland), two broods are not uncommon for those Chiffchaffs which have returned early in the breeding season. At a study site in Switzerland, Schönfeld (1978) found that eight out of 12 pairs were double-brooded in one year and ten out of 11 pairs in the following year. Second broods are generally smaller, with on average three to four eggs being laid. The laying of the second clutch may begin within days (or even less than 24 hours) of the first brood having left the nesting area, or in

An adult female removing a faecal sac after feeding her nestlings. Nest sanitation and concealment from predators is an important requirement.

some cases they may still be on hand (and even expecting to be fed). The behaviour of the adults during the second breeding cycle is much as that during the first. As the season progresses towards July, or slightly later in the month further east, the male, however, becomes more dowdy and the wear of the feathers heavier, and the period spent singing declines to only a few minutes in the early mornings.

The period which young take to reach maturity or independence seems to be slightly longer for second broods than for the young of first broods, with an average of 14–15 days to fledging and a total of 18–19 days to independence. Reasons for this are not particularly clear, but it may be related to the time of the season, availability of food, and the state of the female and the energy required to fulfil the demands of the growing young.

There is very little documented information to show the productivity or breeding success of pairs. In Switzerland, Geissbühler (1954) found that, of 235 eggs laid only 103 actually produced young to the fledging stage. In northern Russia, a four year study by Danilov *et al.* (1984) of 12 nests on the Yamal peninsula found that, of the total of 70 eggs laid, 57 hatched and from these 41 young fledged, giving an overall success rate of 59 per cent; 19 per cent of losses were at the incubation stage (about half of these due to predators) and a further 28 per cent at the fledging stage (where 17 per cent was due to predators and the remainder to bad weather).

11

MIGRATION AND MOVEMENTS

Apart from the sedentary birds living on the Canary Islands, the vast majority of the northern-breeding Chiffchaffs, certainly those to the north of latitude 55°N, move to the south of the breeding range or beyond for the winter. In terms of distance travelled, however, the Chiffchaff is not among the really long-distance species, being easily outdistanced by the Willow Warbler, which forsakes all parts of the Palearctic and its northern breeding range for the tropics, some individuals even going as far south as the southern Cape area of South Africa. The two species slightly overlap in their winter ranges: the southern boundary of the Chiffchaffs winter range, in northern and central Kenya, marks the northern boundary of the Willow Warbler's winter range.

Autumn departures

At the end of the breeding season, when the fully-fledged young have become independent of their parents, the adult birds undergo a complete body, wing and tail moult as part of their preparation for the autumn departure and surviving the winter. The young reared in the summer have dispersed away from the nesting area and are roving solitarily or in loose groups and seemingly at random, through suitable feeding areas, but are familiarizing themselves with the surroundings in order to have somewhere to aim for when returning in the following spring. At this time of year bird life in the northern forests and woods is fairly quiet; adult birds have become shy and unapproachable and the young are quietly going about their business, mostly feeding in the tops of trees.

Following the post-breeding moult (which is undergone by all adults irrespective of whether they have bred) or even while it is in progress, they begin to feed in earnest on the abundance of insects to build up some reserves of body fat in preparation for the long flights of the autumn migration, when food along the way will probably not be available. The normal body weight of an adult Chiffchaff varies depending on the time of year from a low of 5.5 g to about 11.5 g, the latter for birds that have actively fed and fattened up in preparation for the autumn departure. At the end of the breeding period the adults are most likely to be towards the lower end of this weight range, especially the females, which have had the most demanding activity of feeding and rearing at least one and possibly two broods of young. Within a very short space of time, possibly a matter of days, the birds' weight increases. In both Chiffchaffs and Willow

Warblers, most weight is put on very rapidly just prior to departure on spring and autumn migration. The Willow Warbler is the longer-distance migrant and puts on up to 2 g more than the Chiffchaff.

At this time of the year, early August, it is difficult to determine between young birds gradually dispersing from their breeding areas and the first real movements of the southward migration. For the young, it is most probable that dispersal becomes migration within only a matter of days and the distances travelled increase. The main difference is that dispersal away from the breeding area is a daily, gradual, almost random movement from bush to bush, tree to tree or woodland to woodland, with a daily accumulation of miles, while migration in its true sense is, for most small passerines, a strategic nocturnal movement covering distances of probably tens or hundreds of miles away from (or in spring towards) the northern breeding areas and navigating by instinct with an innate compass and map of the northern night sky.

In the British Isles and across Scandinavia, the first real signs of migration are towards the middle of August, when birds are seen moving along hedgerows, lines of hills or the banks of river courses. Within the next two or three weeks there will be a more noticeable passage or arrival of birds at points away from the breeding areas. One of the most exciting facets of autumn migration is that small migrants can occur almost anywhere. They can be seen in any habitat remotely suitable – anywhere where the birds find themselves and there is a chance of snatching an insect or two on the way. As the month of August progresses, more Chiffchaffs are noticeably on the move and snatches of song, in some cases quite prolonged bursts, particularly early in the morning, are heard.

The peak period of departing nominate *collybita* Chiffchaffs from Britain (*abietinus*-type birds do not generally appear in Britain until later in the month, after the peak of departing British breeders) is during the last three weeks of September. The main heading of birds leaving the British Isles seems to be south, with some emphasis towards the south-east of England where the crossing to the Continent is narrower and easier than elsewhere.

During September most of the visible movement through inland Britain will have passed, with the possible exception of individual lingering at one or two particularly good feeding sites. Some spectacular large-scale arrivals, or 'falls', of overnight migrants have occurred at the observatories and prominent coastal points along the south coast of England. These may be multiple arrivals of several species, or on some occasions may just be of Chiffchaffs (or, earlier in the autumn, Willow Warblers) with a few individuals of one or two other migrant species caught up in the movement. Some of these falls of migrant Chiffchaffs have been particularly noteworthy, with maxima of 700 at Beachy Head, Sussex, on 19 September 1989, rising to 2,000 at the same place five days later, 1,000 there on 16 September 1985 and 1,200 on 29 September 1989.

Large numbers can also occur elsewhere. There have been movements involving daily totals of 300 Chiffchaffs on Lundy in the Bristol Channel on 16 September 1958 and 350 on 27 September 1970, which, together with

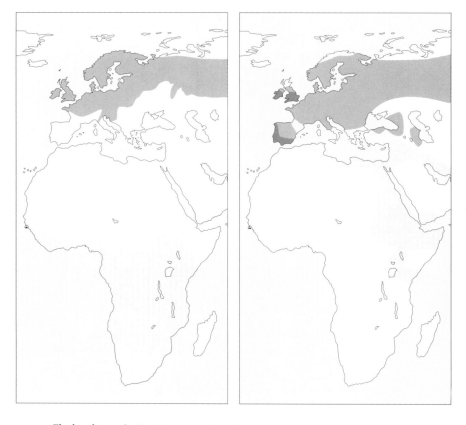

The breeding and wintering ranges of Willow Warblers (left) and Chiffchaffs. The areas overlap in winter in south-west West Africa and northern East Africa.

similar numbers at Portland and at headlands elsewhere in south-west England, are probably of birds leaving Ireland, showing that the movements of departing birds from Britain are not entirely towards or through the south-east. Recoveries of breeding birds ringed previously while on migration show that many from Ireland, the Isle of Man and north-west England move south or south-east before turning south-west or south. That is not, however, to say that some do not move south direct from Ireland to Portugal or even further south, as there are occasional records of these small birds arriving on ships in the eastern Atlantic, such as those in September at the weather station 'Juliet' positioned about 640 km due west of Co. Kerry.

In southern France the peak period of passage is, not unexpectedly, slightly later than the main departure dates from Britain and southern Scandinavia, and continues until the end of October. Further west, in northern Portugal, birds are seen on passage from the end of August, when some have undoubtedly made a direct crossing from Brittany, the British Isles or possibly slightly further east, but the peak period is the middle of October or slightly later. In central and southern Spain, where considerable numbers of the northern-breeding Chiffchaffs winter, there appears to be little appreciable change in the numbers until October (though the first arrivals are actually in late August) when the numbers of the local *brehmii* race are greatly augmented by wintering *collybita*, which remain until the following April. Ringing recoveries of Chiffchaffs wintering in Spain show that many come from (in declining order of numbers of recoveries) Germany, France, British Isles, Netherlands, Switzerland, Italy, Denmark and the former Yugoslavia.

In North Africa, passage occurs from late September to early November, although records from many areas, particularly Morocco, suggest that the Chiffchaff does not become common until the middle of October at the earliest. In southern Algeria, it is abundant at some of the southern oases in October and November, with the situation after these months somewhat confused by the presence of wintering birds. A similar pattern exists in Mauretania, where considerable numbers pass through but wintering birds are not noted before the middle of November or December. In the eastern Canary Islands, migrant Chiffchaffs (the majority being nominate *collybita*) occur on passage from late August and through September, with small numbers after this date involving either migrants or winter visitors.

The earliest date for Chiffchaffs arriving in Senegal is about 20 September, although, curiously, the earliest arrival date for the Gambia is a little over a month later on 25 October. There are first-arrival dates also in late September Mali, Niger and northern Nigeria, although there are also August records in the oases of the southern Sahara, from the northern Aïr province of Niger, which must be of the earliest birds to leave Europe.

In the Middle East, the autumn passage or winter arrival, mostly involving those birds breeding in south-east Europe or slightly further north in central or eastern Europe north to western Poland, is from October to the end of November. In Egypt, Chiffchaffs (which may be *collybita* or *abietinus*, though the latter far outnumbers the former) arrive slightly earlier than in Israel or elsewhere in the Middle East, with passage from late September to late October; this suggests that many make a direct crossing of the Mediterranean, a possibility supported by the record of six birds which came aboard a ship off Alexandria on 3 November 1961.

Ringing recoveries from Cyprus show that many of the Chiffchaffs wintering there breed in western Germany and Poland; other recoveries of birds ringed at breeding sites in Germany, Luxembourg and Belgium show that many (if not most) of the breeding population winter in eastern Spain, southern France and the Balearic Islands. A small number of recoveries, however, reveal that some birds move farther south to winter along the north coasts of Morocco, Algeria and Tunisia. Chiffchaffs from eastern Germany, Poland, Sweden, southern Finland and the Baltic Republics, south to Hungary, which are undoubtedly *abietinus*, move south-east and generally go farther than those in western Europe, as recoveries in Greece,

Bulgaria, Cyprus, Syria, Israel and Egypt reflect. British-ringed Chiffchaffs have also been found in winter southwards into central Morocco and Mauretania and more sparsely in the eastern Canary Isles. There are also several notable recoveries of British and Belgian Chiffchaffs in Senegal, Gambia and Mali. Undoubtedly, many birds from Norway and central Sweden which move south-west in autumn through the British Isles and the Low Countries also winter in much the same area as those from Britain, but as yet the numbers ringed and recovered have been comparativly few compared with those elsewhere in north-west Europe.

In southern Scandinavia and western Russia, the pattern of departure of *abietinus* Chiffchaffs is very similar to that of birds from the British Isles, with passage noted from late August to October with peaks in the last two weeks of September and early October, although passage through the Baltic Republics often continues to mid-October and through Byelorussia to the end of the month. By contrast, most *collybita* have left the western and central European parts of the range (from Switzerland to Hungary) by the middle of September, and from then on most individual migrants seem to be solely *abietinus*.

Southern Lapland is the area of migratory-divide for Chiffchaffs. It separates those going either south-west (on a route through Britain, western and central Europe or south-east through Finland and the Baltic). As with most rules applied to populations of birds, however, there are exceptions. Some birds from Norway and Sweden (which should go south-west) have been recovered in the south-eastern wintering area. Birds from Finland and western Russia (particularly those breeding on the Kola peninsula) have the longest distance to travel: most winter in the Middle East, Saudi Arabia and north-east Africa; one long-distance traveller, which was ringed as a nestling in Finland, was recovered in Uganda .

The northern edge of the wintering area for *abietinus* birds lies from the Dobruja region of south-east Romania to Macedonia and much of Greece, where passage is recorded from mid-August, but the birds remaining in this area for the winter probably do not arrive until later in the autumn.

The advance guard of autumn migrants arrives on Cyprus in early October, or occasionally in late September, with most passage through the island in the period from the middle of October to the end of November. All three races have been recorded on Cyprus, but only *collybita* and *abietinus* are known to occur in any numbers and *tristis* is by far the least common; *abietinus* is undoubtedly the commonest but there are many individuals which are apparently intermediate in characters between *collybita* and *abietinus*, suggesting an area of origin that straddles the respective edges of the range of both races. Migrant and wintering *abietinus* occur in eastern Libya from October onwards and stay until March, with smaller numbers spending the winters in the date palms of Cyrenaica and the desert oases.

The passage of a small number of *abietinus* Chiffchaffs into and through the British Isles usually occurs from mid-October to early November and coincides with the movement of the later-moving *collybita* from the north-eastern areas of the range. This arrival appears to be (depending on the weather conditions) on a fairly wide front, with birds regularly recorded at this time from points as far apart as Fair Isle, Bardsey, the Calf of Man, Spurn and Portland and at many other localities in between (including many inland sites), but is usually less noticeable in south-east England.

About the same time as the arrival of *abietinus* into Britain, a considerable number of *tristis* or *tristis*-type birds occur which are intergrades, or birds from areas of overlap with *abietinus*. This arrival takes place from middle to late October (occasionally in early October in years of predominantly easterly winds in Europe) and is usually first noted in the northern isles or at various points along the east coast. These late migrants are often seen in company with (or arrive at the same time as) other wanderers from Siberia, which can also mean arrivals of Yellow-browed, Pallas's, Radde's or Dusky Warblers. There are annual records of *tristis* (or *tristis*-types) from most of the eastern and southern counties in England and Scotland, or the southern coastal counties of Ireland, of birds on passage or during winter.

In Iceland, the Chiffchaff is among the most frequent of the autumn vagrants; most are of the race *abietinus* and probably of Scandinavian origin. Between 1979 and 1992 there were just over 420 records in autumn, an average of 31 birds per year, and a maximum of 83 in 1980; most of these records are from one site in south-east Iceland and occur in the period from late September to the middle of November.

Chiffchaffs are also regular migrants to the Faroes, with single records for all months except February. Most records are from October to early November and involve *abientus*-types, but there are also three records of *tristis*. (In spring, Chiffchaffs are very scarce in the Faroes, and most individuals show characters of the nominate race.) The annual occurance of these birds is closely influenced by the prevailing weather conditions, with more noted in years of easterly or south-east winds over the North Sea. There is also an old, undated, record of a Chiffchaff from Spitsbergen.

The race *tristis*

Chiffchaffs of the eastern race *tristis*, especially those in the north-east and east of the range, move initially south-west or west into western Siberia before turning south to avoid a direct and potentially extremely hazardous crossing of the great mountain barriers of northern China, Tibet and the Himalayas. Those breeding in north-east Siberia take an almost semicircular route via southern and south-west Siberia to winter in Pakistan or northern India. Some, however, clearly do cross parts of the mountain ranges, as small numbers have been recorded on passage through Sinkiang in north-west China, the western Himalayas and Nepal. Charles Vaurie in his book *Tibet and its Birds* (1972) also gives several records of Chiffchaffs on the central and northern plateaux of Tibet, but he does not specify to which race his data refer. At the time of his writing, in the late 1960s, Mountain Chiffchaff *P. sindianus* was widely considered to be a race of the Chiffchaff; Vaurie gives details of the breeding birds of Tibet and includes references to the possibility of Chiffchaffs breeding in the Kara Kash valley, which (since this is well outside the breeding area of *tristis* Chiffchaffs) is now taken to be a reference to *sindianus*.

A Chiffchaff of the race brehmii showing the slightly longer bill and a brighter green tone to the upperparts.

The departure dates of *tristis* birds from the breeding range cover about the same period, late August and early September, as that of northern breeding *collybita* and most *abietinus*. Some movement in the southern and western part of the range has been noticed in the second half of August and passage through the southern edge of the range also begins in the middle of that month. The last birds to leave the breeding area in the valley of the lower Yenisei have gone by the second week in September and the forests of the central Urals and much of the lowlands of central Siberia are deserted by the middle of the month, with only a few lingering into October. Birds from a huge area of northern Russia move on a broad front through Siberia and west or south-west through Mongolia, which includes a crossing of the Gobi desert, and the upland wastes of Sinkiang in western China to enter the Indian subcontinent via the southern Tien Shan, northern Pakistan, Kashmir and the valleys of the Hindu Kush or (far fewer) to arrive in northern India via Nepal and a route that takes them across the main Himalayan range.

Passage through western Siberia is heaviest in September, coinciding with the movements of *collybita* and *abietinus* to the west. In southern Kazakhstan, the first migrants arrive at the end of August or in early September and passage becomes heavy during the month, by the end of October virtually all birds will have passed through, as there are no records of any wintering in the area. By late September or early October the last birds have left western Siberia shortly after the first hard frosts and just ahead of the first heavy falls of snow.

In Afghanistan, autumn passage begins in mid-September and peaks towards the middle of October, with most having passed through by the last weeks of the month. In Kashmir and Baltistan, the first of the wintering birds arrive in early September and later in the month passage

A winter plumage Chiffchaff of the nominate race wintering in the Middle East. The plumage has become much duller than that in autumn and has not yet moulted into the brighter tones of spring plumage.

becomes quite heavy; the birds press on into southern Pakistan and northern India, where most arrive from the middle of September, with small numbers still arriving through Nepal in late September and early October. In northern Pakistan and throughout much of the Punjab district of north-west India, the Chiffchaff becomes an abundant winter visitor from the middle of October. The passage slows later in October, but some arrive in the valleys of the Hindu Kush in early November. From here, the birds fan out to winter throughout northern India (south to north-west Maharashtra, Madhya Pradesh and southern Bengal), the lowlands of Nepal east to Bhutan (where it is less common) and western Bangladesh.

Further west, Chiffchaffs arrive to winter in Iraq, southern Iran or pass on over the Gulf of Oman in late October or occasionally as early as the end of September to winter in Oman and the eastern provinces of Saudi Arabia. In Bahrain, there is a very light passage from the middle of September which builds into a peak which lasts into early November and small numbers remain to winter. In North Yemen small numbers occur as winter visitors from the middle of November to the middle of April.

The race *brehmii*

Movements of this race are of shorter distance and duration than for any of the three northern races. Moreover, exact movements have been little studied and are, for the most part, obscured by migrants and wintering birds of the nominate race. It seems from the information available that many birds of the race *brehmii* do not leave the Iberian Peninsula but move to lower-lying areas, where they do not breed, and become well distributed throughout the temperate areas, especially around the Mediterranean. The movements of those breeding in North Africa are unclear, but are probably similar distance in pattern. Some individuals of this race have, however, moved, perhaps exceptionally, much farther: there are winter records from Mali in January and from a national park in Ouagadougou, Burkina Faso.

Return movements

The first signs of northward movement or an urge to move are noticeable in European and western Asian Chiffchaffs in late February. Movements over any appreciable distance at this time of year are, to some extent, however, dependent on the prevailing weather patterns, for the more northerly birds are still at risk from heavy falls of snow and freezing temperatures will rapidly suppress any early urges. For the more southerly winterers in West Africa, the first signs of spring migration are birds on passage through the western Sahara from the middle of February. In the desert oases of southern Algeria and south-east Morocco, the passage of birds from wintering areas further south is noticeable in late February and March, about a month earlier than the departure of those which have wintered in the oases of the western Sahara. By the middle of April most of Chiffchaffs wintering in southern West Africa will have left (a few individuals linger into early May in the Gambia and there are records of birds remaining in Mali throughout the northern summer), and this is reflected by passage along the coast of north-west Africa and through the eastern Canary Islands in March and early April, though some individuals, particularly those which appear to be *abietinus*-types, can still be seen on passage in May. Movement through Tunisia is from February to the middle of April, but the majority of birds have passed through by the middle of March. By the end of April few Chiffchaffs, certainly those of the nominate race, remain in North Africa. The majority of the population, mostly males, will by this time be on their breeding grounds and establishing territories.

The northward routes in spring are almost the exact reverse of the southward journeys in autumn, but information on the numbers on passage at points around the Mediterranean suggests that the distances travelled in a single flight are much longer. In places such as Gibraltar, Sicily and Malta, far fewer Chiffchaffs are seen on spring passage than in autumn, and this is due to birds pushing on into the heartland of southern and central Europe before making a landfall. The urge to move north and establish breeding territory is clearly a much greater stimulus for a host of passerines such as these small warblers, which may need to compete for territorial space and the favours of the later-arriving females.

Passage through the western Mediterranean and into southern Europe seems to be on a fairly broad front, with birds arriving in Spain, France, Corsica, Italy, Sicily and Cyprus from the middle of February and most passing through from early March to mid-April. The first to arrive back in Switzerland are singing in early March and the main arrival of breeding birds follows soon after, with late arrivals up to the end of April. In southern Germany the average arrival date is about 30 March, but this can vary from year to year by up to ten days either side of this – largely determined by the temperatures in late winter. It is also most likely that the Chiffchaffs arriving back early on their breeding territories, in southern and central Europe, have spent the winter no further away than the shores of the Mediterranean.

The first singing Chiffchaffs in Britain can usually be heard in the first half of March but again this is seemingly determined by the severity of the weather, with some, perhaps in exceptional years, singing in southern England and Ireland in the last four or five days of February. The origin of these early birds is complicated by the presence of local wintering individuals, which, although they may have been present for a few days or weeks before the arrival of the first songsters, tend to wander away (particularly on mild and warm days) from the wintering areas, and we know little about how far or how fast they return to their breeding areas. Some (if not most) are of Continental origin, as shown by a bird ringed in Belgium in late October 1982 and retrapped 472 km west two and a half months later in Hampshire at the beginning of January 1983. It is probably fair to assume that most February birds have wintered locally and are making short-distance movements back to their nesting areas.

From the records kept by observatories around the coast of Britain, it can be seen that the first Chiffchaffs return in early March. Arrivals are noted from the Isles of Scilly to Dungeness in Kent and in some years as far north as Skokholm and the Calf of Man. As with arrivals in the Mediterranean, the first birds are just as likely to be seen or heard at an inland gravel pit, wood, copse or hedgerow as in a bush on a prominent headland, which again reflects the broad front of the arrival and the urge to press on inland without dallying at points along the coast.

Irish Chiffchaffs arrive from early March, but only in very small numbers, and this may reflect either a relatively local origin or that they have travelled only a short distance, possibly from an original point north of the Mediterranean. Most arrive in the first half of May, when daily totals of up to 200 have been recorded at Hook Head or Great Saltee; on one exceptional date in mid-May there were up to 600 at the latter site. These dates are about a month later than the period of heavy passage through south-west England, and possibly result from a more southerly wintering area or a slightly delayed passage compared with those breeding in or passing through England. It is also interesting to note that most Chiffchaffs arrive in Ireland via the south-east corner, again reflecting the main passage routes over the western approaches into south-west England.

In sharp contrast to the predominant direction taken by departing Chiffchaffs in autumn, when coastal observatories and headlands in south-east England record the highest numbers, the peaks in spring are found in south-west England at various points from the Isles of Scilly to Portland Bill. Daily maxima here in spring have regularly been around 150, and passage continues through the whole of April and into early May. Further east along the south coast of England numbers are usually much lower at this time of year, with daily totals normally in the region of between 20 and 50; notable exceptions include 100 at Dungeness in mid-April 1975 and a huge arrival of over 800 Willow Warblers and Chiffchaffs in mid-April 1970 at Beachy Head, Sussex, where there have been similar daily arrivals of between 200 and 300 birds in subsequent years.

In some years when the weather is mild, small numbers of late or lingering migrants are recorded up to mid-June in northern Scotland and the Outer Hebrides (including St Kilda). Some of these may be lost, but they quite often sing and defend territories. It is presumably only the lack of a female that prevents breeding taking place; many of these birds which arrive late may not have been in breeding conditions earlier, but they may also represent the means by which the species is able to expand its range.

In central and northern Europe most Chiffchaffs are heading north at much the same time as the species is moving into Britain. In southern Scandinavia, the first arrive usually in the last ten days of March, and most passage takes place from early April to early June, with a noticeable peak in early May. Further east and north, most movements concern solely birds of the race *abietinus*; through the Balkans and central eastern Europe and western Russia mostly from late March to the end of April. In southern Finland and east to the Moscow region and north to around Archangel, Chiffchaffs do not arrive until mid-April and passage lasts into early June, when there are still a few birds passing, presumably to the more northerly breeding localities.

In Turkey, early migrants arrive in the Ankara area in early March and most birds pass through the country in early April, with daily totals of over 200 noted on several occasions at certain locations. Passage through the Caucasus is from the end of March, but again most do not pass through the area until early or mid-April. In the Ukraine, passage begins at much the same time as elsewhere on the same latitude, but the peak is often a week later, a few days after the middle of the month. Those birds which breed in the northernmost parts of the range in central and northern Siberia arrive in early May, but the majority are not establishing territories before the end of the month. In particularly wet springs, migrants frequently pause or delay moving on into the bad weather around the Caspian Sea, in some years remaining as late as the end of May.

The first departing *tristis* Chiffchaffs from the plains of northern India, Pakistan and Iran are on the move from early March, and by early May only the last lingering stragglers are still in northern India. Several authors have commented on finding Chiffchaffs at quite high altitudes on spring passage through the western Himalayas. Roberts (1992) found them abundant at up to 2830 m in the Murree hills in early May, and Whitehead before him found them common at up to 1500 m in Kohat district of northern Pakistan at the same time of the year. In northern Afghanistan the northward passage is heaviest from the middle of April, while slightly further north, through the plains and deserts of Central Asia, Chiffchaffs become common migrants throughout March and most have passed through by the end of April.

In western Siberia, the first returning birds are seen in mid-April and the main arrival follows about a month later; arrivals continue over much

Confusion or look-alike species.

Bonelli's Warbler
1st winter

Bonelli's Warbler
adult autumn

Radde's Warbler
1st winter

Dusky Warbler
1st winter

Booted Warbler
1st winter

Booted Warbler
1st winter (varia)

Booted
Warbler
spring

of the Siberian breeding area to the end of May and the first week of June. In middle or late May the first individuals appear in the lower Pechora and Kolyma river basins and other areas of the same latitude, while in the remote northern and north-eastern parts of the range, particularly along the Yenisei river above the Arctic Circle, the first are seen in late May but most do not arrive until early or even the middle of June.

Occurrence of vagrants

Migrating individuals which have overshot their summer or winter destinations are always a strong possibility, as they are at the mercy of prevailing winds and driven by the urge to move on to their intended goal. We have already noted above that *abietinus* is a regular vagrant to Iceland and the Faroes. Chiffchaffs (of unknown race) have been recorded from Bear Island and Madeira. In the latter locality, Bannerman (1965) cited records in December (twice) and February, all from around the turn of the century; since the species is a migrant to North Africa and winters in small numbers on the eastern Canary Islands, however, it has, probably, occurred far more often in Madeira but been overlooked.

Records of true vagrancy by Chiffchaffs, or of individuals considerably outside the normal area of occurrence, are very few and far between, unlike the situation with several other members of the genus which regularly navigate wrongly or migrate in the opposite direction to the one in which they should go. The most surprising records of Chiffchaffs are those from eastern and southern China: two birds of the race *tristis* have occurred in Hong Kong, the first in March 1986 and the second two years later in December 1988.

Wintering Chiffchaffs in West Africa appear to be faithful to their area and are rare further south into Ghana and much of central and southern Nigeria. The species has been recorded as an exceptional or very scarce visitor to Cameroon, and in central Africa it is possibly regular in Zaïre, but very little information has been published to confirm this.

Speed of migration

Most of the data available suggest that Chiffchaffs migrate mostly by short-stage flights. This is purely speculative, since at present we have only a fairly rudimentary (but continually improving) idea of individual flight ranges of small passerines. The collective evidence built up from several sources using both ringing recoveries and known crossing distances and arrival times of migrants of a whole range of unidentified passerines, indicates movements both small and large, depending on the terrain to be crossed along the route.

Initial departures are made either singly or in flocks from areas where individuals have congregated to await the right conditions in the night sky for departure. Birds of several species of small passerines tend to depart loosely together and maintain a loose uniform pattern of movement in the same direction. Pictures from radar screens have shown that on clear nights, when conditions for nocturnal movement are good, there is a mass of birds of many species on the move. Some of these movements do not necessarily depart from coastal areas or headlands offering the shortest sea crossing but may be from further away, while other migrants depart from the south coast of England for a comparatively short crossing to France or northern Spain. A study of visible migration is, in the main, restricted to watching birds arriving or departing from certain observation points (usually coastal headlands) along the routes used by the migrating birds. Since most passerines are nocturnal migrants, however, watching them actually on the move is a fairly rare phenomenon.

It seems most likely that Chiffchaffs, at least those of the nominate race, move in relatively short stages of between 80 and 120 km at a time when crossing land. They are, however, equally capable of much bigger distances, as movements across the northern North Sea from Scandinavia and across the western parts of the English Channel show that these small birds of about 10 g or slightly less can have individual migration stages of between 500 and 800 km. This is calculated by using a theoretical flight time of seven hours at an average flying speed of about 45–55 kph, although it has to be admitted that since our knowledge of maintained flight speeds and the duration of flights still depends on a fair element of guesswork, this estimate possibly contains a fair margin of error.

Information gained from ringing recoveries, both in Britain and in Europe, reflects a range of flight duration times. Those Chiffchaffs heading south of the Sahara can move from Britain to Senegal in a matter of days, as a bird ringed in Wiltshire in late August 1991 was recovered in Senegal two and a half months later, which if undertaken in daily flying times equates to an average of 50 km a day (undoubtedly the individual flights were much longer and combined with days of resting before the next stage). Better evidence that Chiffchaffs are capable of sustained flight for a considerable period is shown by the recovery of a bird in Latvia in October 1981, 31 hours after it had been ringed in Ottenby, Sweden, a distance of at least 287 km. Another Chiffchaff ringed at Castricum in the Netherlands on the last day of October 1989 was retrapped six days later on North Ronaldsay in Orkney, a distance of 874 km in a direct line. If the bird had flown this line at a daily average speed, it would have had to maintain an average distance of about 200 km per day, but, since the majority of this route is over the inhospitable North Sea, it is conceivable that the journey was undertaken with only one or perhaps two stops along the way.

There are interesting comparisons to be drawn with similar recoveries. A Willow Warbler ringed on the Calf of Man in April 1988 was recovered the next morning at Copeland, Ireland, an overnight flight of 84 km. In his book on the Redstart, John Buxton gives some flights and distances covered by that species on migration: one bird ringed on Heligoland, Germany, was recovered in Finland 14 days later and had covered the distance of 2450 km at an average speed of 175 km a day; another, also ringed on Heligoland in the autumn, was recovered 2050 km away in southern Portugal five days later and had covered the distance at an average speed of 410 km a day.

12

MORTALITY AND LENGTH OF LIFE

The oldest known Chiffchaff was at least seven years and one month from the time of ringing to when it was found dead in France in 1969, but as it was an adult when ringed (in April 1962) it is most likely that this bird was probably at least ten months older. This is quite a remarkable achievement for such a small passerine. Small migrant songbirds are usually fairly short-lived and most are lucky to survive beyond their first year. Most Chiffchaffs, certainly of the migrant races, probably live long enough to reproduce once and replace themselves or, in years of abundant food supply, produce sufficient offspring to lead to an overall increase in the population, which ultimately leads to an expansion of the range. Such range expansions are not, of course, dependent soley on or influenced purely by the survival of large numbers, as there are other factors such as climate, food supply and levels of predation which have a bearing.

Information from ringing recoveries also reveals a considerable, perhaps surprising, number of Chiffchaffs in their third and fourth years which are still, apparently, going strong. Several of these have involved birds which were ringed in Britain or central Europe during the breeding season and caught in subsequent years either in their winter quarters in Senegal or somewhere on migration along the way. Information obtained by ringing and subsequent recovery shows that most are likely to be recaught in their first or second year of life; thereafter the chances of retrapping a longer-lived bird decline quite markedly (because there are fewer of them). Of 2850 Chiffchaffs trapped in Malta, 5.2 per cent were retrapped in their first year after ringing, 2 per cent in their second year and 0.55 per cent, 0.45 per cent, 0.24 per cent and 0.07 per cent in their third to sixth year of life respectively. We have very few details of the annual survival rates of Chiffchaffs and precious little material exists on comparable species. Work carried out on Willow Warblers in Russia in the 1980s has shown an annual mortality of adults of 65-76 per cent, which is probably an average figure for a small migrant species. The figure for first-year birds is likely to be much higher, since the trials and tribulations of life in the first six months to one year take a very high toll of the population.

Undoubtedly one of the factors which greatly influences the number of adults surviving to breed is the long journey undertaken twice a year between summer and winter grounds and back again. We know very little of the mortality toll that migration takes for any species, especially one that crosses large areas of water or inhospitable terrain. From the annual rates of surviving birds, we can gauge that at least half of the population of most small warblers succumbs to the forces placed upon it during migration. While we know of the preparation undertaken by the birds to put on sufficient fuel reserves in the form of fat for the journey, we know very little of what margin exists for error or for encountering bad or unfavourable weather along the way.

Birds crossing large areas of land (as do possibly most of the Chiffchaffs breeding in Europe and Asia) are able to put down on any convenient piece of land when the conditions for onward travel become inhospitable. But what of those which become lost or disorientated in thick cloud or sea fog and move out over large stretches of sea or deserts or mountains where there is no likelihood of shelter or replenishment of fuel should the reserves run out? In such cases – and our knowledge of how often this happens is particularly sparse – it is clear that individuals which have neither the strength nor ability to divert around these conditions become casualties. Is this also the fate of birds which for one reason or another have imperfect or faulty navigational clocks and move the wrong way on a compass bearing that takes them through west or even north-west Europe instead of south or south-east and into southern Europe, North Africa or the Middle East? What is the fate of those Chiffchaffs from Scandinavia or further east in northern Europe which occur every year in Iceland or those which have strayed as far from the normal migration routes as Bear Island and Spitsbergen? What also of the birds that are swept out over the Atlantic when moving south out of Britain and north-west out of Europe in autumn, such as those that occurred in September 1959 at the weather station 'Juliett' stationed in the eastern Atlantic approximately 640 km west of Co. Kerry, Ireland, and 1280 km due south of Iceland?

Anyone who has spent time at coastal bird observatories, headlands or peninsulas in spring or autumn will be familiar with the sight of birds arriving in the early hours of dawn. Equally familiar will be the sight of tired or even exhausted migrants in bushes or whatever vegetation is afforded; in some cases they are so tired that they are past caring about the proximity of humans. These are birds on the very edge of their reserves, and some will have probably passed the levels from which they can recover and will probably perish in the following night. Unless the bird can refuel quickly and without a great expenditure of further energy, it is likely that it will not survive long. The birds we see arriving may be just the small remainder of the total that departed when the weather conditions for onward movement seemed favourable but later changed (when the birds had left or when they were over large areas of water).

Not only do weather patterns influence and affect birds on migration, but poor or wet weather during spring and early summer is liable to result in a very poor breeding season, ground-nesting birds suffer an appallingly high casualty rate in extremely wet summers or even in particularly severe summer storms. Early migrants heading north to establish territory are also at very high risk of encountering severe late-winter weather, especially the further north they travel.

Most early-spring weather is characterized by warm sunny days of light southerly winds and clear skies. The same clear skies also lead to

plunging temperatures at night and heavy frosts. Early migrants such as the Chiffchaff frequently react to these early bursts of warm weather and the temporary presence of a plentiful supply of food, and undertake short movements away from their winter quarters. At little notice these periods of fine weather are replaced by more dominant low-pressure systems or rapidly-moving high-pressure systems, which pass quickly across Britain and are followed by prolonged periods of intensely cold northerly winds which bring spells of severe frost and snow to parts of Britain and much of northern and central Europe. In late April 1950, a heavy snowfall over much of England and Wales resulted in the deaths of many early migrants. Many of the Chiffchaffs which had moved north at their usual time and by then had established territories were wiped out as a consequence: on one farm alone in southwest Wales A. K. Kent (1951) found 13 dead Chiffchaffs in a small alder and willow copse about 0.1 ha in extent.

As noted in Chapter 3, perhaps the second most influential factor on the success, stability or failure of the populations of northern migrants heading into tropical Africa for the winter is the rainfall in the Sahel region of the southern Sahara. For certain species which are heavily dependent on this area for the winter or as a temporary refuelling stop-over, the annual rainfall is crucial to their survival. We have no estimates of the size of the Chiffchaff population that is reliant on this area, but previous droughts or poor rainfall levels there have had severe consequences for the numbers returning to breed in Britain and elsewhere in northern Europe. Although not solely responsible for declines in Chiffchaff populations, the poor rainfall years in the Sahel, such as the period in the early to mid 1970s and again in 1984, corresponded with sudden crashes in the numbers returning to breed – by as much as 50 per cent of the previous breeding population in some areas.

Predation

Predation of both adults and young also accounts for a fairly high loss of birds. On their breeding territories, the adults are vulnerable to attacks from predators such as Sparrowhawks and possibly to a lesser degree Kestrels. In his extensive monograph on the Sparrowhawk, Ian Newton (1986) records that Willow Warblers breeding on farmland and in forest plantations provide up to 2.4 per cent of the prey items of a pair of breeding hawks and it is likely that in some areas this could apply to a similar extent to Chiffchaffs.

More problematic for such ground-nesting birds is predation on eggs and nests by stoats, weasels and rats. There is no precise information on the level of predation by these animals, but it is probably extremely extensive as they are all widely distributed throughout the range of the Chiffchaff in Britain. Crows, and particularly Magpies, are probably also responsible for the destruction or abandonment of many nests; again, we have little idea of the level of predation (although crows in general are not so adept at finding nests hidden in vegetation). Once out of the nest, newly-fledged birds risk falling prey to any of these opportunistic predators, and the chances of a full brood of young Chiffchaffs (or any other small ground-nesting songbird) reaching maturity are vey small.

The effect of humans

More indirectly, the trappings of man's existence have caused many problems and taken a toll on the bird. Untold numbers are killed by such seemingly innocent structures as power lines, roadside telegraph wires, high TV or radio aerials, greenhouses and, in recent years, buildings with reflective or mirrored glass, which seem to have an inexplicable attraction for the birds. Higher numbers are undoubtedly killed by the cars we drive and the pets, particularly cats, we keep. Although not especially a threat to the Chiffchaff, the domestic cat is probably a much greater threat to many of our small songbirds than is generally appreciated.

The hand of man has clearly had a considerable impact on the amount of available breeding habitat there is for Chiffchaffs in Britain and much of central and northern Europe. The destruction of the ancient forest has had an untold effect on the present levels of the population. The species and its habitat are not unduly threatened, but its particular requirements could easily be affected if there were radical changes in forestry and agricultural policies and procedures in the future. The conservation movement, which has gained considerable ground in Britain and Europe since the 1950's, has ensured (not always intentionally or solely for the Chiffchaff) the future of many Chiffchaff breeding strongholds, and in the British Isles and much of the western parts of the range the species would seem to have a virtually assured future. The same is probably true in the vast areas occupied by the races *abietinus* and *tristis*, since (for the foreseeable future at least) their habitat still exists in plenty.

Select Bibliography

Ash, J.S., Hope Jones, P., and Melville, R., 'The contamination of birds with pollen and other substances', *British Birds* 54 (1961), 93–106

Bannerman, D.A., *Birds of the Atlantic Islands*, Edinburgh, Vol. 1. (1963), Vol. 2 (1965)

Batten, L.A., and Wood, J.H., 'Iberian Chiffchaff at the Brent Reservoir', *London Bird Report* 37 (1974), 78

Beven, G., 'Pre-Coitional display of Chiffchaff', *British Birds* 39 (1946), 246–247

Beven, G., 'Changes in breeding bird populations of an Oakwood on Bookham Common, Surrey, over twenty seven years', *London Naturalist* 51 (1976), 7–19

Browne, P.W.P., 'Palearctic birds wintering in SW Mauretania, Species distributions and population estimates', *Malimbus* 4 (1982), 69–92

Clark, J.M., and Eyre, J.A., *Birds of Hampshire*, Hampshire Ornithological Society, (1993)

Conder, P.J., and Keighley, J., 'The leg colouration of the Willow Warbler and Chiffchaff', *British Birds* 43 (1950), 238–240

Cramp, S., et al., *The Birds of the Western Palearctic. Vols. VI and VII*, Oxford University Press, Oxford, 1992 and 1993.

Danilov, N.N., Ryzhanovski, V.N., and Ryabitsev, V.K., *Ptitsy Yamala*, Moscow, (1984)

Dementiev, G.P., and Gladkov, N.A. et al., *Birds of the Soviet Union, Vol. 6*, Jerusalem, (1951–4)

Dennis, M.K., 'Wintering Blackcaps and Chiffchaffs in the London Area', *London Bird Report* (1992), 145–152

Flint, P.R., and Stewart, P.F., 'The Birds of Cyprus' (revised edition), *BOU Check-list No. 6*. (1992).

Frost, R.A., 'Phylloscopus warbler with songs of Chiffchaff and Willow Warbler', *British Birds* 79 (1986), 340–341

Geissbuhler, W., 'Beitrag zur biologie des Zilpzalps, Phylloscopus collybita', (1954), *Orn. Beob.* 51 (1954), 71–99

Gibbons, D.W., Reid, J.B., and Chapman, R.A., *The New Atlas of Breeding Birds in Britain and Ireland: 1988-1991*, Poyser, London, (1993)

Glutz von Blotzheim, U.N., and Bauer, K.M., *Handbuch der Vogel Mitteleuropas. Vol. 3*. Wiesbaden, (1991)

Goodman, S.M., and Meininger, P.L., et al., *The Birds of Egypt*, Oxford University Press, Oxford, (1989)

Gwinner, E., 'Beobachtungen uber die aufzucht und jugendentwicklung des Weidenlaubsangers (Phylloscopus collybita)', *J. Orn* 102 (1961), 1–23

Haftorn, S., 'Willow Warbler Phylloscopus trochilus imitating the song of the Chiffchaff P. collybita', *Bull. B.O.C.* 113 (1993), 216–224

Heard, C.D.R., 'Racial identification of wintering Chiffchaffs', *Birding World* 2 (1989), 60–65

Herald, D.G., and Johnson, I.A., 'Chiffchaffs in the Dale Peninsula, Pembrokeshire', *Nature in Wales* 11 (1968), 116–121

Homann, P., 'Beitrag zer verhaltensbiologie des Weidenlaubsangers (Phylloscopus collybita)', *J. Orn.* 101 (1960), 195–224

Howard, E., *The British Warblers; A history with problems of their lives*, London, (1908)

King, J.R., 'Song by female Phylloscopus warblers: the influence of 'stress'', *British Birds* 6 (1992), 73–74

Kozlova, E.V., 'The Birds of Southwest Transbaikalia, Northern Mongolia and the Central Gobi. Part V', *Ibis* (1933), 301–330

Lack, P., *The Atlas of Wintering Birds in Britain and Ireland*, Poyser, Calton, (1986)

Lovegrove, R., Williams, G., and Williams, I., *Birds in Wales*, Poyser, London, (1994)

Madge, S.C., 'Field identification of Radde's and Dusky Warblers', *British Birds* 12 (1987), 595–603

Munroe, B.L., and Sibley, C.G., *A World Checklist of Birds* Yale University Press, New Haven, (1993)

da Prato, S.R.D., and E.S., 'Post-juvenile moult in relation to dispersal and migration in the Chiffchaff Phylloscopus collybita', *Ringing & Migration* 12 (1990), 80–85

Penhallurick, R.D., 'Chiffchaffs wintering at sewage-works in west Cornwall', *British Birds* 71 (1978), 183–186

Price, M.P., 'Notes on population problems and territorial habits of Chiffchaffs and Willow Warblers', *British Birds* 29 (1935), 158–166

Price, M.P., 'Warbler fluctuations in oak woodland in the Severn Valley', *British Birds* 54 (1961), 100–106

Schonfeld, M., *Der Weidenlaubsanger*, Wittenberg Lutherstasdt, (1980)

Saether, B.E., 'Habitat selection, foraging niches and horizontal spacing of Willow Warbler Phylloscopus trochilus and Chiffchaff P. collybita in an area of sympatry', *Ibis* 125 (1983), 24–32

Sharrock, J.T.R., *The Atlas of Breeding Birds in Britain and Ireland*, British Trust for Ornithology, Tring, (1976)

Simms, E., *British Warblers*, Collins, London, (1985)

Svensson, L., *Identification Guide to European Passerines*, 4th edition, Stockholm, (1992)

Thom, V., *Birds in Scotland*, Poyser, Calton, (1986)

Tiainen, J., 'Nestling growth in three Phylloscopus warblers in Finland', *Ornis Fennica* 55 (1978), 1–15

Ticehurst, C.B., *A Systematic Review of the Genus Phylloscopus*, London, (1938)

Vaurie, C., 'Systematic Notes on Palearctic Birds. No. 9 Sylviinae: the Genus Phylloscopus', *Am. Mus. Novitates* No. 1685 (1954)

Williamson, K., '"Northern Chiffchaffs' and their area of origin', *British Birds* 47 (1954) 49–58.

Williamson, K., 'Nomenclature and origin of 'northern' Chiffchaffs', *British Birds* 48 (1955), 561–562

Williamson, K., 'Identification for Ringers', *The Genus Phylloscopus*. Vol. 2. (1974) British Trust for Ornithology

Witherby, H.F., Jourdain, F.C.R., Ticehurst, N.F., and Tucker, B.W., *The Handbook of British Birds*, 5 vols. Witherby, London

Appendix of Scientific Names

White Stork *Cicinia ciconia*
Glossy Ibis *Plegadis falcinellus*
Garganey *Anas querquedula*
Sparrowhawk *Accipiter nisus*
Kestrel *Falco tinnunculus*
Corncrake *Crex crex*
Ringed Plover *Charadrius hiaticula*
Temminck's Stint *Calidris temminckii*
Curlew *Numenius arquata*
Marsh Sandpiper *Tringa stagnatilis*
Snipe *Gallinago gallinago*
Kittiwake *Rissa tridactyla*
Arctic Tern *Sterna paradisaea*
Cuckoo *Cuculus canorus*
Hoopoe *Upupa epops*
Sand Martin *Riparia riparia*
Swallow *Hirundo rustica*
Tree Pipit *Anthus trivialis*
Red-throated Pipit *Anthus cervinus*
Yellow Wagtail *Motacilla flava*
Wren *Troglodytes troglodytes*
Dunnock *Prunella modularis*
Robin *Erithacus rubecula*
Nightingale *Luscinia megarhynchos*
Redstart *Phoenicurus phoenicurus*
Blackbird *Turdus merula*
Song Thrush *Turdus philomelos*
Mistle Thrush *Turdus viscivorus*
Savi's Warbler *Locustella luscinioides*
Cetti's Warbler *Cettia cetti*
Sedge Warbler *Acrocephalus schoenobaenus*
Marsh Warbler *Acrocephalus palustris*
Reed Warbler *Acrocephalus scirpaceus*
Booted Warbler *Hippolais caligata*

Garden Warbler *Sylvia borin*
Lesser Whitethroat *Sylvia curruca*
Whitethroat *Sylvia communis*
Blackcap *Sylvia atricapilla*
Bonelli's Warbler *Phylloscopus bonelli*
Wood Warbler *Phylloscopus sibilatrix*
Willow Warbler *Phylloscopus trochilus*
Mountain Chiffchaff *Phylloscopus sindianus*
Plain Leaf Warbler *Phylloscopus neglectus*
Radde's Warbler *Phylloscopus schwarzi*
Dusky Warbler *Phylloscopus fuscatus*
Smoky Warbler *Phylloscopus fuligiventer*
Arctic Warbler *Phylloscopus borealis*
Greenish Warbler *Phylloscopus trochiloides*
Two-barred Greenish Warbler *Phylloscopus plumbeitarsus*
Green Warbler *Phylloscopus nitidus*
Yellow-browed Warbler *Phylloscopus inornatus*
Pallas's Warbler *Phylloscopus proregulus*
Goldcrest *Regulus regulus*
Firecrest *Regulus ignicapillus*
Spotted Flycatcher *Muscicapa striata*
Blue Tit *Parus caeruleus*
Coal Tit *Parus ater*
Red-backed Shrike *Lanius collurio*
Magpie *Pica pica*
Jay *Garrulus glandarius*
Chough *Pyrrhocorax pyrrhocorax*
House Sparrow *Passer domesticus*
Chaffinch *Fringilla coelebs*
Twite *Carduelis flavirostris*
Crossbill *Loxia curvirostra*

Index

Page numbers in italics
refer to illustrations

125

NATURAL HISTORY BOOKS

A complete range of Hamlyn Natural History titles is available from all good bookshops or by mail order direct from the publisher. Payment can be made by credit card or cheque/postal order in the following ways:

BY PHONE
Phone through your order on our special *Credit Card Hotline* on **01933 414 000**. Speak to our customer service team during office hours (9 a.m. to 5 p.m.) or leave a message on the answer machine, quoting your full credit card number plus expiry date and your full name and address. Please also quote the reference number J405N12C.

BY POST
Simply fill out the order form below (photocopies are acceptable) and send it with your payment to:
Cash Sales Department,
Reed Book Services Ltd.,
P.O. Box 5,
Rushden,
Northants, NN10 6YX

J405N12C

I wish to order the following titles:

	ISBN	Price	Quantity	Total
Hamlyn Guide to the Birds of Britain and Europe	0 600 57492 X	£8.99	....	£.......
Photographic Guide to Birds of Britain and Europe	0 600 57861 5	£9.99	....	£.......
Where to Watch Birds in Britain and Europe	0 600 58007 5	£12.99	....	£.......
Hamlyn Species Guide: The Kestrel	0 540 01278 5	£12.99	....	£.......
Hamlyn Species Guide: The Barn Owl	0 600 57949 2	£12.99	....	£.......

Add £2.00 for postage and packing if your order is worth £10.00 or less   £.......

Grand Total £.......

Name _____ (block capitals)

Address _____

_____ Postcode _____

I enclose a cheque/postal order for £ _____ made payable to Reed Book Services Ltd
or
Please debit my ☐ Access   ☐ Visa   ☐ American Express   ☐ Diners

account number ☐☐☐☐ ☐☐☐☐ ☐☐☐☐ ☐☐☐☐

by £ _____ Expiry date _____ Signature _____

SPECIAL OFFER: FREE POSTAGE AND PACKAGING FOR ALL ORDERS OVER £10.00, add £2.00 for p+p if your order is £10.00 or less.

Whilst every effort is made to keep our prices low, the publisher reserves the right to increase the prices at short notice.
Your order will be dispatched within 5 days, but please allow up to 28 days for delivery, subject to availability.
Registered office: Michelin House, 81 Fulham Road, London SW3 6RB.
Registered in England no 1974080.

If you do not wish your name to be used by other carefully selected organizations for promotional purposes, please tick this box ☐